Raising your internet business

How to deliver successful web projects for your small business

By Clive Verrall

Copyright 2018 Clive Verrall

http://www.cliveverrall.com

This e-book is licensed for your personal enjoyment only. This e-book may not be re-sold or given away to other people. If you would like to share this book with another person, please purchase an additional copy for each person. If you're reading this book and did not purchase it, or it was not purchased for your use only, then please return to the website and purchase your own copy. No part of this publication may be reproduced, distributed, or transmitted in any form or by any means, including photocopying, recording, or other electronic or mechanical methods, without the prior written permission of the author, except in the case of brief quotations embodied in critical reviews and certain other non-commercial uses permitted by copyright law. Thank you for respecting the hard work of this author.

~~~

Preface

Do you want your business to be among many businesses that thrive and expand due to their successful online business models? Many of these businesses derive the majority of their revenues from internet customers whom the businesses will never meet or from customers who find the businesses online and then visit the businesses' physical premises. How do these businesses attract these customers? These opportunities are only possible if your business has an online presence.

How do I put my business online? What services should I offer? How will I accomplish all of this on a small business budget? You may have a vision of the website you would like to have, but as a small business owner you probably won't have an IT department to which you can delegate this project responsibility. You can hire experts to help you, but you won't know how to supervise them unless you first gain an understanding of the key subjects involved. How can you negotiate a good deal unless you already know the advantages and pitfalls of putting your business online?

As a web professional I have regularly been asked these questions by my myriad clients. Usually I only have time to give clients a quick answer, and not enough time to really explain everything I'd like. This book contains the more comprehensive answers that I would like to have told my clients, and from which any small business reader can now benefit. Put all these explanations together, and this book gives you the essential information you need to get your business online.

In my career I have built many websites to put businesses of all sizes online, starting with my first commercial website in 1997, through to recently founding Coconut Tickets (a specialist event e-ticketing platform). In addition, as the host of a Meetup group for business start-ups, and as a small business owner myself, I have encountered and overcome nearly the whole range of small businesses challenges in the digital world.

~~

Contents

1. Are you making the most of online opportunities? 1
2. From opportunities to projects 3
   - What to do first 3
   - Deciding on your business strategy 4
   - Online strategy 6
   - Web projects 6
3. Online business models 7
   - Selecting the right business model 7
   - Business information website 7
   - Affiliate marketing 8
   - Drop shipping 10
   - Online store 12
   - Digital store 14
   - Online travel booking 15
   - Online event ticketing 16
   - Membership websites 17
   - Online learning 18
   - Online auctions 19
   - Online advertising 20
   - Software as a Service (SaaS) 22
   - Lead generation 24
4. How much will I need to invest? 25
   - Price points 25

These will increase your project costs...27

Will your website have a high number of visitors? 28

Will your website have a unique business model that's never been seen before? 28

Will there be a lot of automation? 28

Do you need to offer a wide variety of payment methods? 28

Will your website be very graphical? 29

Will your website need "application" features? 29

Long Term Investment..29

5. Your website project 31

Website projects step by step 31

Define your business requirements 32

Business analysis 32

Design the solution...32

Build the solution 34

Test 35

Deploy to your hosting environment 35

Improve and iterate..38

6. Can I do the web project myself?...39

What does it mean to do it yourself?...39

Define your website requirements...39

Business analysis 39

Designing the solution..40

Building the solution...40

Testing 41

Deployment to your hosting environment...41

Training you and your team 41
Conclusion 41

7. Who can help me? 43
   Web developer 43
   Web designer 44
   SEO expert 45
   Website project manager 46
   Web security expert 46
   Web professional 47

8. Choose the right domain name 48
   What is the purpose of a domain name? 48
   The importance of branding 49
   Domain extensions 49
   Choosing your domain name 52
   Buying your domain name 54
   Domain privacy 55

9. Should I use WordPress? 57
   Small business website revolution 57
   Why is WordPress often chosen? 57
   What are people using WordPress for? 58
   Evolving your use of WordPress 59
   8 reasons not to use WordPress 60

10. The rise of website builders 63
    What is a do-it-yourself website builder? 63
    Website builders by market share 64
    Advantages of website builders 64

Disadvantages of website builders 65

Conclusion on website builders 67

11. How to choose the right technology 68

Efficient use of this chapter 68

Static business information websites 68

Dynamic business information websites 69

Blog 70

E-commerce 70

High performance e-commerce 71

E-booking 73

12. Choose the right payment gateway provider 74

Payment Automation 74

Are online payments the right solution for your business? 74

The cost of online payments 74

Online payment market share 75

PayPal 76

Stripe 77

High risk online payment 78

Where to host your website 79

Economy shared hosting 80

Premium shared web hosting 80

Virtual Private Server (VPS) 81

Managed VPS 82

Dedicated server 83

Deploying new versions of the website; 83

VPS technical support 84

Hosting market leaders 85
WordPress managed hosting 86
13. Can all your customers use your website? 87
The main browsers on the desktop by market share are: 87
These are the most used browsers on smart phones: 88
14. How to connect with your online customers 89
How can your prospects ask questions? 89
Contact us 89
Website live chat 89
15. Regulations that can't be ignored 92
Are there any online regulations? 92
Identification 92
Data protection and privacy 92
PCI DSS 93
European General Data Protection Regulation (GDPR) 95
Consumer protection 97
Accessibility and discrimination 98
Anti-spam laws 99
Collecting taxes 100
Copyrights, trademarks and patents 100
Protection of minors 101
Advertising and marketing 102
People's Republic of China 104
16. Is your website secure? 106
Very real security risks 106
Attacks are often not human 107

    Login attacks 108

    Software vulnerabilities 108

    Shared hosting attacks 109

    Denial of service attacks 109

    What can you do to improve security? 110

17.   Your digital marketing strategy 112

    Organic search and SEO 113

    Content marketing 116

    Email marketing 117

18.   Increase visitors with social media marketing 120

    Purpose 120

    Advantages 122

    Disadvantages 123

19.   Get visitors with online paid advertising 125

    Why advertise online? 125

    Search engine advertising 126

    Social media paid advertising 128

    Online display advertising 130

    Advert re-targeting 131

20.   Improve online success with analytics 132

    Why use analytics? 132

    Website interaction 133

    Website replay 134

    Social media interaction 136

    Search engine information 136

21.   How to engage digital professionals 138

Who do you need to hire?..138

Where can these people be found? 141

Hiring on freelance websites 142

22. How to work with your web team...147

Remote working 147

Signs of trouble to come 150

23. We went live—what happens next? 153

View your analytics..153

Look for errors...153

Data maintenance 155

Check if you have these five ticking time bombs 155

24. Case studies 157

Business information website 157

Event Ticketing 158

3D printing store..160

25. Glossary 163

26. About the Author..168

27. Acknowledgements 169

28. Other books by this author..170

~~

1. Are you making the most of online opportunities?

Have you ever wondered what being on the internet can do for your business? What business models can the internet support? What opportunities could the internet open up for you?

Popular internet business models that are within reach for your business include:

Business information website(s) to generate leads and help customers find your physical store;

Online store(s) to increase revenues selling your physical products online;

Digital store(s) to increase revenues selling digital products online;

Online booking to sell services and tickets online;

Membership websites;

Online learning;

Online auctions;

Automated services to improve efficiency, reduce costs and increase sales;

Content marketing to communicate your business's expertise and authority;

Online networking to connect with leads and funnel them towards a sale;

Online advertising;

Software as a Service (SaaS);

Lead generation.

If you are not taking advantage of these models then your business may be missing out. This book aims to explain what these business models are, what it will take to build the website your business needs to take advantage of these models and the many opportunities the internet offers.

2. From opportunities to projects

What to do first

If your business wants to realize the limitless opportunities made possible by online services, then the first thing you need is a clear definition of the target you want to achieve and a plan that will define the path to this new business target. The plan will differ depending on whether you have an existing business that you want to put on the internet or whether you are starting a new business. This book aims to cover both cases and will point out when a different approach needs to be taken if you have an existing business.

The best way to get started is to decide what business your are going to do online (your digital business strategy), then to identify the business model that most closely matches what your business intentions are. This will allow you to define the website(s) you need (this is your online strategy) and then the project(s) you will need to deliver. Following that you can dig deeper into these projects; identify the technologies needed, estimate the costs involved and therefore the investment you will need to make. At the next level of detail you can estimate the human and technical resources needed to achieve each of your projects and finally estimate the time-line for all projects required. This book will help you think about these steps on your own and help you to identify outside help that could help you with the planning (e.g. a website project manager) as well as the implementation.

The following diagram summarises the recommended steps.

Online business planning
1. Define digital strategy
2. Identify online business model
3. Define the projects
4. Choose the technologies
5. Draft investment estimate
6. Find project resources
7. Draw project timelines
8. Improve investment estimate
9. Start the projects

You don't need to complete one step entirely before moving on to the next step. In practice you may iterate through some steps until you can complete all the steps.

This advice may sound somewhat stuffy and theoretical when all you want to do is start building a website and getting customers. However, making strategic decisions and planning the work that needs to be done will help you to reach your goals, to communicate instructions to others and to evaluate whether what you have invested in is really working or not.

Deciding on your business strategy

Your digital strategy is how your business plans to operate in the digital economy, in other words it is a statement on what your business is going to do on the internet in order to make money. If you have an existing business then the he digital strategy explains how digital technologies (e.g. a website) will be applied to your existing business and/or how the enablement of new business capabilities will be achieved using these digital technologies.

The following diagram summarises the common ingredients of your digital strategy:

- Digital Strategy
- Online Business Models
- Planned Products
- Planned Services
- Customer Intelligence
- Digital Sales Strategy
- Dig Marketing Strategy
- Transformation Strategy
- Online Strategy

Your digital strategy could simply be applying new technologies and the internet to your existing business; or rather it could be using new technologies (and the opportunities they create) to completely transform your existing business. For example, you could decide to track your customers' use of your digital services and use the resulting data to refine your existing business model and/or deploy resources. This is referred to as using "Big Data" to derive customer intelligence that then feeds your digital strategy.

This sub-section is just an overview. You may need to read through the subsequent chapters as well before you feel ready to generate your own digital strategy.

Most importantly, the real result of your digital strategy is the profit that you make from your online sales. Generating a digital strategy is an important early step for communicating within your business team and investors, but it is not in and of itself the final goal.

Online strategy

Your online strategy is the customer-facing part of your new business on the Internet, and includes the website(s), mobile app(s) and the email communication(s) you will create.

You may have already decided what you need to do online, in which case you can use the rest of this book to validate your online strategy and pick up useful tips along the way. Alternatively, you may need to read the whole of this book, and get the full picture before deciding precisely what you need to do online. Either way, we all know that everything costs time and money, so be sure that your chosen online strategy matches your business model and is within your budget.

Web projects

The lion's share of your online strategy will comprise the implementation of your web project and methods for marketing the project to your customers. Consequently, these topics will be covered in great detail throughout the rest of this book.

3. Online business models

Selecting the right business model

One important element needed to define how your business within your digital strategy is the selection of the online business models that you will employ.

This chapter will explore the online business models available to small businesses. Your final digital strategy might utilize one of these business models, or even something custom that incorporates various elements from different online business models.

Business information website

Creating a business information website is often the first step a business takes towards becoming part of the world of online business (the digital economy). Once completed, a business information website tells potential customers everything they need to know about your business in order to buy your products and services. The goal of the business information website is for customers to make contact, which may include:

To visit your physical store(s);

To place an order by email or telephone;

To ask for a quote;/or

To know what products and services your business offers.

It may seem like all of your competitors already have business information websites, thus if your business does not have one then as a first step creating a business information website can be incredibly effective.

Having this type of internet presence can enable your business to:

Be found through online searches by business category;

Be found online by physical location (e.g. printing shops near me);

Communicate business hours (opening/closing times);

Market your products and services;

Demonstrate authority in your field of products and services.

In other words, you can use the business information website to generate leads for your business that you can then convert to sales in your physical store or by phone.

If you follow good responsive web design practices then your business information website will also be accessible to smart phone users. This additional accessibility is incredibly powerful when someone is already in your neighbourhood, has already decided to make a purchase and is simply looking for a physical store in which to spend their money. Specifically, potential customers in the vicinity of your physical store can use their smart phones to not only find your business, but also to locate your physical store using your business information website and Google Maps. More online searches now take place on smart phones each day than on desktops, so the mobile audience is one that most online businesses should not ignore.

Affiliate marketing

Affiliate marketing is a revenue-sharing business model. An affiliate marketing business promotes the products (or services) of a third-party merchant, and takes a share of the third-party merchant's revenue when the promotion leads to a purchase.

Raising your internet business

Affiliate Marketing

The key enabler for affiliate marketing is the website of the affiliate marketing business. Visitors are drawn to the affiliate marketer's website through organic web searches and referrals, with additional traffic coming from returning customers.

Skill is required to create an online presence that is easily discoverable and that offers product information in such an attractive way as to convert visitors into third-party merchant sales. Typically this means writing your own review of a product that is tailored to fit with your audience, rather than copying existing content (e.g., the official description written on the product's packaging) related to the product.

The actual sale of the product or service is made on the third-party merchant's website—not on the affiliate marketer's website. Therefore, while affiliate marketing may sound similar to e-commerce, there is a big difference in that an affiliate marketing website does not usually require the technical complexity of an e-commerce website. Clicking a button on the affiliate marketer's website simply redirects a visitor to complete his or her purchase on a third-party merchant's website.

For affiliate marketing to work there needs to be a formal agreement between the affiliate marketer and the third-party merchant on (i) what products/services will be sold, (ii) the amount of commission that will be paid to the affiliate and (iii) how the commission will be paid.

Marketing and website design are the key skills required to start an affiliate marketing business. Also, if someone already has a website with a good number of regular visitors then adding affiliate marketing for related products and services can be a good route towards monetizing that existing website.

By way of an example, consider the sale of books about fishing. If someone already has a popular website about fishing that many people regularly visit, then the website owner could make money from that website by selling books about fishing using an affiliate model. To achieve this, the website owner could simply add a books page to the website showing a catalogue of books. When a visitor to the website clicks on one of the books in the catalogue the visitor is redirected to Amazon to purchase the book. Amazon would then pay commission for such sales to the website owner (now an affiliate marketer) on a regular basis. The affiliate marketer does not need to pay any money upfront to buy books as stock or to package/ship the books.

There are many ways in which an affiliate marketing website may attract visitors, with models including:

Product price comparison websites;

Product review websites;

Coupon and price discount websites;

Charity websites;

Themed websites (e.g. fishing);

Personal websites.

Drop shipping

Drop shipping is a type of e-commerce which requires an online store showcasing the products. Customers can select a product and pay for it online. Unlike in affiliate marketing, the purchase of a product actually takes place on a drop shipper's website. Therefore, a drop shipping website requires complete e-commerce online payment capabilities.

Drop Shipping Model

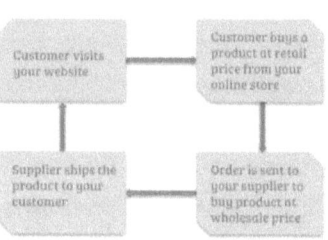

However, unlike a traditional e-commerce store, a drop shipper does not hold products in inventory, nor does a drop shipper ship products himself. Instead the drop shipper will use a supplier (e.g., wholesaler) that is prepared to ship small quantities of products to the drop shipper's customer at the drop shipper's request.

The advantage for a drop shipper is that he or she requires less cash than a full e-commerce store, because the drop shipper does not need to buy or store products in advance (i.e., before knowing if he or she will be able to sell the products). A drop shipper saves not only the cost of a warehouse to hold inventory (the drop shipper never receives or holds the goods), but also the cost of staff to pack physical products and pass products to a courier service (the drop shipper does not himself ship products). As a result, a drop shipper reduces his or her overall investment and corresponding risks.

There are, of course, disadvantages to drop shipping as well. The main disadvantage is the extra transaction cost of drop shipping. Because a drop shipper relies on a supplier to store products and to send products on-demand to the drop shipper's customers, the price paid by the drop shipper to the supplier to fill a customer order will be higher than the price paid by an e-commerce store to the supplier for a bulk order of products shipped to the store's warehouse. In practice, the supplier to the drop shipper may not be the original manufacturer of the product, and as result will be adding the cost of warehouse and shipping service to the cost of each product. Often the price paid by the end customer to the drop shipper for a product will be higher than the price of the same product if purchased from an e-commerce store competitor.

With the risks associated with often having to sell products at higher prices than bigger (e-commerce store) competitors, a drop shipping business needs to be especially good at marketing to draw potential customers to its website and make sales.

Online store

An online store is a full e-commerce store for selling physical products online. Products are purchased in advance from a supplier (e.g., wholesaler or original manufacturer) and stored in the store's warehouse. The online store's website will show customers all the products the store has to offer. On the online store website, products can be selected and placed in an electronic shopping basket (shopping cart) before the customer takes the shopping basket to the website's checkout. At the checkout, the products are paid for using an electronic payment facility such as PayPal or a credit card processor such as Stripe. Once payment has been made, the online store will then package the products and ship them from its own warehouse to the customer (often using a third-party courier service).

Typically the customer pays the online store the price of each product, as well as the cost for shipping products to the customer's chosen delivery address. During payment there may also be an opportunity to enter a discount code that has been supplied by the online store as an incentive to buy from the store.

Digital marketing is key to getting visitors to the online store, and the use of multiple marketing channels is normal. Once a visitor is on the website, the design of the store will be a strong factor in converting the visitor into a customer. Often online stores that are competing in a crowded market place will also use paid internet advertising to increase the number of visitors to their store.

Online stores can be categorized as being either:

Business to customer (B2C), or

Business to business (B2B).

Most online stores follow the B2C model—retail websites that sell directly to their end customers. There are also many successful B2B online stores that facilitate the sale of products to other businesses.

Depending on the products being sold, an online store may need to offer many variations of each product from which the customer can choose. For example, an online clothing store may offer many different styles of jumpers for sale. If the customer wishes to buy a jumper then the customer will need to select the style, the colour and the size of that jumper. This is, of course, an exact mirror of a physical store selling jumpers. However, it is worth bearing in mind that these product variations increase the complexity of the e-commerce website and add to the required inventory stored at the warehouse.

Digital store

A variant of an online store is a digital store (or "digital media store"). All the products sold at this type of store are digital products. These are virtual products that do not require a warehouse for storage nor a physical shipping facility.

Digital Store

Customer views your website shop

Customer orders product from your website and pays electronically

Customer downloads purchased product from your website

Similar to an online store, the digital store comprises a website that displays a catalogue of all the products on sale. The customer selects products that he wants, places them in a virtual shopping basket and then pays for them at the checkout. Once payment has been received, all the products in the basket will be available to the customer for immediate download from the digital store. This is noticeably different from an online store, wherein the customer has to wait for physical products to be physically packaged and delivered.

Types of products sold by a digital store can include:

E-books;

Software;

Music;

Photos;

Videos;

Audio books.

Online travel booking

Online travel booking allows a customer to book accommodation, flights and travel packages completely online. The online booking website will display a whole catalogue of travel services that can be booked. The visitor to the website can select services, choose locations, enter dates and a number of travellers to obtain an immediate online quote. If the visitor accepts the quote then the chosen package can be put in a virtual shopping basket and paid for online. Next, an electronic confirmation of the purchase, and possibly electronic tickets, are delivered to the customer by e-mail.

Online travel booking

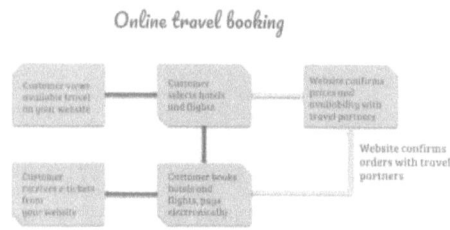

Some travel websites are more sophisticated than others in the way that they sell their products online. The simplest kind of travel booking is that in which the inventory of services and availability is managed only within the website itself. Therefore there is no need to check availability with any third-party suppliers before allowing a booking to be purchased on the website. The next level of sophistication is that in which booking can take place for services requiring third-party supplier confirmation before making a booking on the website (or in which third party suppliers have a way to update the availability of services on the website). Finally, the greatest complexity is found in fully-automated online travel booking that checks availability and makes bookings immediately with third-party suppliers (e.g., purchasing airline reservations from an online agent, which is extremely complicated because it requires integration with official airline booking systems—airline connectivity projects are lengthy and likely to require approval of your system by third-party suppliers before they are authorized to make any sales).

While airline booking systems are generally quite Spartan, allowing customers to book tickets as simply as possible, by comparison niche travel booking websites are likely to have much more content. To attract visitors, niche travel booking websites must offer something that the airlines themselves do not. For example, niche travel booking websites are likely to give away free online information that adds value for their customers, such as articles about travel, travel blogs and lots of images of destinations and hotels. Accordingly, the website for a niche travel booking company can require considerably more design effort, as well as frequent high-quality content creation.

Online event ticketing

The business model for online event ticketing is one in which an event manager uses a website to sell tickets to his or her event online. The event manager can choose if visitors to the website will be able to see a catalogue of all events available from the manager, or just the one specific event that is being promoted. A visitor can then select the event(s) he wishes to attend and choose the ticket types, dates and quantities (e.g. 2 adult tickets). These selected tickets are placed into a virtual shopping cart after which the visitor can continue shopping for more tickets or go to the website checkout and pay for the tickets. Once payment has been received by the website the electronic tickets will be issued to the customer by email.

Online Event Ticketing

On the day of the event the event manager's staff will ask to see the electronic tickets of everyone that arrives at the event. Typically there will be a QR code or barcode on each electronic ticket. The event staff will have a hand held tool to read and validate the tickets before letting the ticket holders into the event.

For example, let us consider online booking for a music event. The visitor searches for the event he wants to book online, selects the event, then chooses 1 family ticket and 1 adult ticket. Next, the visitor advances to the checkout, where he pays for his tickets using PayPal and a few minutes later receives an email with his electronic tickets. When he attends the music event, his electronic tickets are scanned at the entrance, and once his tickets are validated he is allowed to enter the music event.

Membership websites

If you have valuable information then that information could be sold to people online for a fee. The information would be made available as part of a website, and people would be asked to pay to gain access to that web content. Often this is the online equivalent of the many information services that are already available via physical delivery in the traditional economy.

A fairly simple example is that of an electronic newspaper. The pages of the newspaper become the pages of a website, but if a new visitor tries to view those pages then he would find that he cannot get access. To read the electronic newspaper a visitor needs to pay a monthly fee and thereby become a subscriber to the service. Once he is a subscriber then he can access any page(s) of the electronic newspaper for as long as his subscription is active, and the newspaper's content is continually updated by the newspaper company. The electronic newspaper's business model is selling as many subscriptions as possible, and keeping subscribers for the long-term by providing high-quality and regularly-updated, content. This online business model is a simple type of membership website.

A more complex example is that of a membership website that offers different levels (tiers) of membership subscription plans. For example, there may be a free membership level which allows a member access to only a small number of documents and pages, while additional paid membership levels (e.g. bronze, silver and gold memberships) would each allow a member access to greater amounts of content on the website. The content on such a membership website is likely to be something valuable that would have taken considerable resources to put together (e.g., business competitor or stock market analysis reports).

Online learning

A learning management system (LMS) is like an online electronic college implemented as a website for learning skills online. An LMS is designed to cover the complete process of learning a skill, including:

showing which courses are available;

allowing new students to register for courses;

delivering those courses to the student online;

tracking students' progress;

facilitating communication between students and teachers;

facilitating communication between students in the same courses;

testing the students' knowledge;

issuing completion certificates.

All of these processes are achieved online using the LMS, normally without any need for intervention from staff.

Students pay for the courses for which they register. Typically only online payment is accepted.

The learning material is often delivered in the form of either a slide show presentation with a voice over from the teacher, or a video lecture. In the case of a slide show, the content may also include video clips wherein the teacher can demonstrate how he would tackle a problem.

Increasingly, students want an interactive learning experience wherein they can validate what they are learning with other people. This experience can be achieved by offering students an online forum in which to discuss the course with fellow students and teachers.

Online auctions

Online auctions are e-commerce websites wherein the price of the goods sold is dependent on the bids people make online during the course of the auction. The online auction allows all interested parties (bidders) to place bids during a specific period of time. When a winning bid is accepted, the associated bidder pays for the goods online and the goods are shipped to him.

The online auction business makes money by providing the auction platform and charging a fee to the seller for a successful sale.

Different types of online auctions include:

English auctions;

Dutch auctions;

Sealed bid auctions.

The English auction is the type of auction most often found online. With this type of auction the price of goods starts low, and bidders place successively higher bids. Everyone involved in the auction can see each amount bid without knowing who placed the bid. When the auction time period expires the person having made the highest bid is the winner (unless this bid is lower than a reserve price which has to be reached). The winner then pays the price he bid and receives the goods.

English Online Auction

A Dutch auction works in reverse. The price starts high and is slowly reduced until a buyer bids that price. The highest bid is the winner, and the winning bidder then pays the price he bid and receives the goods.

With a sealed bid auction no bidder knows how much other bidders have bid, or if they bid at all. Each interested party (bidder) makes one bid for the amount that they are willing to pay. When the bidding time has expired then the highest bid wins, and the associated bidder pays the price he bid and receives the goods.

Online auctions are described as being customer to customer (C2C), because they allow customers to register as sellers to sell their goods to other customers through the online auction platform. The website only provides a platform to facilitate auctions, and does not generally sell goods of its own.

The company eBay is the most famous online auction website, with net revenue of nearly USD 9 billion in 2016. However, the online auction market is quite disjointed, with eBay having less than 50% market share, and accordingly many competitors.

Online advertising

If you already have a website with a large number of regular visitors then you could make money from this website by selling advertising space on your website. The space you offer could be for text adverts or banner adverts with images, audio and/or video.

An advertiser wants people to click on its advert, and for those people to be automatically redirected to its website, where people could purchase a product or service related to the advert. Accordingly, an advertiser will only be interested in buying advertising space on your website if you already have a large number of visitors on the website, and if your website's content is relevant, in one way or another, to the adverts being displayed.

It is important to know what type of adverts will be displayed on your website. People visit your website for a reason, and displaying irrelevant adverts will put people off visiting your website. If you lose your audience then ultimately advertisers will not want to use your website either. So it is a good idea to have adverts that complement your website. For example, if you have a blog website covering performance cars then you may get good results when displaying performance car related adverts.

There are three main ways in which you can be paid for the adverts on your website:

Payment for each impression;

Payment for each click;

Payment on each final sale.

With payment for each impression you will receive money every time the advert is displayed on your website regardless of whether the display of that advert leads to a real sale for the advertiser, or even a visit to the advertiser's website.

Payment for each click is where you get paid every time someone clicks on any of the adverts on your website. Once a visitor clicks an advert they get redirected to the advertiser's website. The advertiser will pay you regardless of whether the click of the advert leads to a real sale for the advertiser.

Alternatively, with payment on each final sale an advertiser pays you whenever a visitor to your website sees and clicks on the advertiser's advert and eventually purchases the product or service being advertised.

The amount you might get paid for each impression will be very small because the advertiser is expecting a very low conversion rate from advert impressions to sales. The payment for clicks will be higher than for impressions, because there will be far fewer clicks than impressions. If you are paid for each sale then your payment from the advertiser will be a percentage of the value of the sale and therefore could be significant, but of course there will be far fewer sales than clicks or impressions.

There are two ways to engage advertisers on your website. One method is simply to find businesses yourself that want to advertise. With this method you will have to set the advert prices yourself, and you can choose which pricing model you want to use. An alternative is to use an established online advertising network. Once you have signed up with such a network then you can paste some code into the advertising spaces on your website and the advertising network will then automatically push its own adverts through onto your website. The most well-known online advertising network is Google AdSense. The downside of using an advertising network is that you have less control over the adverts than if you sell the advertising space yourself, and you must accept the advert pricing dictated by the advertising network.

Software as a Service (SaaS)

The Software as a Service business model is one in which subscribers are charged money for access to centrally hosted software. Typically this software is made available to the subscriber through a standard web browser, and not as a download (the latter is more common in the digital store model).

Advantages of buying a SaaS subscription instead of buying the equivalent software include:

No lengthy downloads or complicated installation of software;

No need to update the software (as that happens centrally);

Software costs are spread out with monthly payments;

Subscriptions can be cancelled.

The price for using SaaS may be a simple flat monthly fee, a flat fee for a certain number of users, or a metered cost dependant on the subscriber's use of the software during the previous month. Also the software may be offered with different features, with each feature having an associated cost. Yet another possibility is that the pricing is dependent on the level of support the user has requested, for example someone that expects to need a lot of support will pay a higher price for greater support time.

Examples of successful SaaS delivered through a browser include:

Customer Relationship Management (CRM) platforms;

Accounting platforms;

Event ticketing platforms;

Online conferencing tools;

Personal finance tools;

Office productivity tools (e.g. Google Apps).

To understand how to deliver SaaS through a browser, it can be useful to consider the online strategy for a SaaS business model to comprise two separate websites. The first website is the public website that everyone can see, which is used to market the service to potential customers, telling them everything they need to know in order to sign-up for the service. The second website is used to deliver the service, and is only accessible to subscribers of the service. The public website is no different from a business information website, however the service delivery website could be very large and complex. The pages that subscribers see might look simple, but behind the scenes there would have been a serious software engineering effort required to build the product that is the "software" of the SaaS platform.

Lead generation

A relatively new business model is the online identification and sale of leads to business clients. The lead generation business will use websites, emails and marketing skills to attract potential customers as sales leads. The business then sell these leads in bulk to clients for a fixed fee per lead.

A lead generation business may run many different lead generation campaigns at the same time, one for each of its different clients.

4. How much will I need to invest?

To help formulate a practical digital strategy, you will need to know how much money you will need to invest. To avoid wasting your time, this chapter aims to give you a general overview of web project costs before discussing the details. Ultimately, your final investment is something that you won't know until you have made key strategic decisions and met with the external professionals you need to help you.

Price points

We probably have all heard stories of businesses that have only paid $200 to put their business online. We probably also have heard of other businesses spending $100,000 or more to implement their digital strategies online. How can there be such a cost variation? Not every business has the same target, and not every business is at the same stage in its life cycle, therefore costs are inherently going to vary a lot. Costs will vary by country and also by language (for anything other than English) but these price points can still be used to get an indicative cost.

To give you an idea of what you can get for you money, below is a sanitized list of real online projects together with the approximate investment amounts that were required to deliver them.

$200 – your own "do it yourself" (DIY) business information website.

$1000 – WordPress business information website built by a freelancer, while you yourself write the copy.

$2000 – basic e-commerce store built by a freelancer using existing tools (e.g. WordPress/WooCommerce or Shopify), while you maintain the content.

$5000 – professional e-commerce store or membership website.

$10,000 – business information website built by a reputable digital agency.

$20,000 – professional e-commerce store built by a reputable digital agency.

$30,000 – bespoke custom online booking system built by a freelancer.

$100,000 – a clone of the Amazon.com e-commerce store (with much lower sales volumes).

$1 million – an e-commerce store that can compete with Amazon.com or eBay (with comparable sales volumes).

$10+ million – actual investments made by the owners of Amazon.com or eBay.

From your own experiences you may believe you can achieve the same project for less money or know that your requirements are such that the price points here seem low. However, the main purpose of sharing these project costs is to introduce real price points that demonstrate that there is a huge range of possible investment amounts. Big businesses spend a lot of money to implement their successful digital strategies. The good news is that we can compete at much lower costs now that they have pioneered the way forward. Most small business owners will not be re-inventing the internet with their online business, but instead will be benefiting from the advances already made by their competitors.

The next point to realise from these price points is that you will get what you pay for. You may be able to get an amazing deal through a friend referring the web professional who built their website, but this will not be possible for everyone.

One strategy would be to start your new online business with an entry level solution, knowing that if your sales volumes increase that you will need to spend more. In this way you can evaluate the success of your digital strategy before committing to a large investment. Nevertheless, you will need to remember that this entry level solution is probably not your final solution, and that you probably need to invest more to support increased sales. This is worth thinking about in advance, so that when you achieve business success you are ready to invest in the next phase of your digital strategy rather than being frustrated at how the cheap entry level solution you built is no longer fit for purpose.

In the world of websites and bespoke software solutions it is normal for the cost of the first delivery of a new solution to be proposed as a fixed price. This is good for you because you can then budget for this fixed amount. However, you need to understand the constraints imposed by a fixed price contract (regardless of whether it is verbal or written). For instance, most freelancers working for a fixed price expect a limited number of revisions to their work, so if you come up with corrections and changes every day for a month then you may receive unexpected invoices on top of the agreed fixed price.

After the website has been accepted, it goes live and any immediate problems are fixed. Any further work will be outside the scope of that fixed price contract, because once you accepted the website, you accepted the website "as is" and the freelancer's initial commitment was complete. You will then be billed for ongoing changes at the freelancer's maintenance rate. Expect freelancers to be much cheaper than digital agencies. For example, in 2017 the global average for a WordPress freelancer was $50/hour, whereas there were reports of well-known agencies charging $100/hour and more for similar work.

When the website is live, if you have major changes to make, or enough small changes that can be bundled into one project, then you can once again request a fixed price from your freelancer (or digital agency).

These will increase your project costs

Answering yes to any of the questions in this section is likely to increase the cost of your project beyond the price points listed in the previous section.

Will your website have a high number of visitors?

If we look again at the "Price points" section we see that higher volume solutions cost more money. This is no surprise, because more time needs to be spent on design, off-the-shelf components can no longer be used, and more complex solutions requiring more custom software need to be built. Therefore, if you forecast anything more than 5000 visitors per day, or plan to process more than 2000 sales per day, then expect the cost of your website to increase compared to the lower volume price points listed earlier in this chapter.

Will your website have a unique business model that's never been seen before?

Doing something unique, like having a unique online business model, could also result in not being able to use off-the-shelf components, which will increase your website costs. In practice, this is worth discussing with an expert professional whom you trust, because (if you are lucky) what you believe is unique may simply be a minor configuration change to the expert and therefore will not require a significant cost increase.

Will there be a lot of automation?

Bespoke automation or integration can increase costs. If you want to connect something to your website that isn't requested very often then you are likely to need a bespoke software solution. Or if you want to control something external through your website then that too is likely to require a bespoke solution. Integration and automation can be time consuming to get right, therefore costs and delivery time-scales will increase. However, the automation or integration you require could have a standard off-the-shelf solution, in which case it may not be overly expensive to add.

Do you need to offer a wide variety of payment methods?

Card payments online look the same from website to website, but unfortunately each payment gateway works differently. There is no standard for how these gateways should work. Therefore adding a large number of different payment gateways to your website is likely to increase your costs significantly. Even if off-the-shelf solutions can be found, payment gateways are complex and making payments correctly is critical, therefore the amount of testing required will also increase. These factors will increase the cost of the project.

Will your website be very graphical?

Very graphical websites will require a significant amount of a web designer's time. Creating graphics and web content is bespoke work, and as such will increase your costs. Similarly, adding lots of data driven graphical charts will take extra time, and increase your costs.

Will your website need "application" features?

What seems like a simple website may require some application features that will increase the cost. For example, you may have a speciality e-commerce store, in which to help customers buy your products you offer an online tool to calculate how much of the products they need (e.g. how much paint they need to cover a room)—this online calculator is really a web application, and is likely to be a bespoke solution for your speciality business (i.e., not something available off-the-shelf).

Long Term Investment

This chapter has focussed on the investment needed to build a website that delivers your chosen business model. To get the full picture of your likely investment it is necessary to consider the yearly recurring costs too.

Yearly running costs could include:

Hosting fees;

Domain registration fees;

Any premium plugin or software licences;

Technical support fees;

Outsourced SEO fees;

Outsourced content management fees;

Website maintenance fees;

You may not choose to outsource or subcontract any SEO or content management (to be explained in later chapters), in which case you will not incur these fees. Similarly, you may not need any additional technical support beyond that offered by the hosting provider in your monthly package fee.

Website maintenance fees are quite likely because problems with the website will be identified (or new issues will arise) long after it is delivered and these issues will need to be resolved by your web developers.

5. Your website project

Website projects step by step

The plan for your online business will include one or more website projects. Decades of research have gone into how technology projects should be organised to deliver business benefits; what they should include and what phases they should have.

This research is not just relevant to big companies, but is also applicable to small businesses. The phases described below may sound like they require an army of people, however the basic model is applicable to website projects of all sizes—anything from one to one hundred people. In practice you may find that the completion of a particular phase is so fast that you may not notice it, however, following the model ensures that nothing gets missed.

There is a risk associated with skipping any of the steps presented here.

The project phases are are summarised in the following diagram.

Project Phases	
1	Define The Requirements
2	Business Analysis
3	Design The Solution
4	Build The Solution
5	Test
6	Deploy Hosting Environment
7	Training
8	Technical Support
9	Improve And Iterate

In the next sections of this chapter we will examine these phases in more detail.

Define your business requirements

For the first phase, write down in business terms what the website needs to be able to do to achieve your online strategy. This can be quite high level; for example implement an online clothes store website with stock management. If it needs to be detailed then this should be because the business problem is detailed. The temptation to go into technical details should be avoided until at least the business analysis has been conducted.

Business analysis

This phase is where you define how your business works or will work with your online solution. If you are building a business information website then the business analysis will include identifying the type of information that you will present on the website. Alternatively, if you are building an e-commerce website then the business analysis will include identifying the types of products that you are going to sell and how your business will fulfil each order.

Design the solution

With the strategy and analysis work complete, you will have enough information to start designing the solution. There are many aspects to this for an online web solution, see the summary diagram below.

Design Solution	
1	User Interaction Design
2	Graphical Design
3	Sales Copy
4	Logical Design
5	Physical Design

There are different parts to designing the solution. If your vision is more complicated than a business information website or a simple blog then you will need technical design. Unless you already have extensive website software experience then you will probably need to hire a professional to generate this technical design.

The first stage is to decide how the users (customers) will use your website. This is where you need to think of every action that the user needs to be perform. It should be quite high level.

Next the graphical design deals with what the user will see for each of these documented interactions with the website. How the customers will see the website is often referred to as the page design. Designing website pages requires a specialist skill set that includes a combination of website knowledge, graphical design and information theory. On a small project it is possible to choose from a selection of pre-made web design templates instead of designing from scratch. However, a pre-made template will be limited in how it can be branded with company information and how unique it can be (e.g., the same template maybe used by another 50,000 websites).

For a more complex website with additional functionality (such as forms, buttons and some application functionality) page designs would normally be delivered to you for approval before website construction starts. The designs may perfectly reflect how each page will look (with the correct colours, spacing and fonts); or the designs could be higher-level illustrations showing the information blocks that will be displayed on each page.

Typically your page design or graphical design makes no attempt to include compelling calls to action. The space to write your sales copy is usually left blank and the next step in the process is to write that sales copy. Because the sales copy is written by different people to the graphical design it may not be exactly step number 3 but, of course, it does need to be complete before the website is finished.

The logical design covers the software components that to go together to make your solution. If you were building a simple business information website then the logical design maybe so simple as to be not necessary to document. In contrast to this, if you were building an Amazon competitor then this stage would be very important.

Finally the last step is the physical design. This is the design of the tangible parts of the solution such as servers and networks. Once again, if this was a solution for a simple business information website then the physical design may simply be need for a shared hosting platform. In which case this step could be completed in minutes. In comparison, the physical design for a leading e-commerce solution may take up many pages.

Build the solution

With the design phase complete you can start to build the solution. This phase follows closely the aspects of the design phase.

User interaction flow is built into the menus, buttons and links;

Making the website pages, creating images;

Entering the sales copy into the pages;

Developing the software components (or connecting pre-made components);

Building and connecting the databases, servers and firewalls.

Throughout these build steps the web developer should be testing what has been implemented. Continuous testing reduces the risk of discovering issues late on in the build process that are then time consuming to fix. This type of testing is not the same as testing in explained in the next section and both types of testing are needed.

During the build phase it is also advisable to have the developer show you what has been built as soon as there is something to see. As long as you can ignore what has not been built, then seeing what has been built so far will help you identify any misunderstanding

Test

When the website is built then the next step is to validate that it works as expected. There are two major categories of testing: the first is the technical team's own testing (mentioned above), and the second stage is termed "user acceptance testing". As the small business owner, you (and your team) must conduct the user acceptance testing. Once you have accepted the product then the technical supplier has achieved his delivery and, contractually, can request payment. Therefore it is very important that the user acceptance testing is conducted rigorously.

For user acceptance testing the best approach is for you to try to use the website as your business's customers would. This is testing both the implementation of the design by the technical team and whether the original design was really fit for its business purpose. Very likely the first version of your website isn't completely right, and needs to be changed and tested again. Building modern websites is complicated, therefore even if the design was good the first version of the website is likely to have some things that don't work or look out of place. Testing and fixing problems is an iterative process wherein you aim to have progressively less and less issues in each round of testing until the website works well enough that it can be used by the intended visitors.

Deploy to your hosting environment

The finished software then needs to be installed on the target hosting environment. This complete act is referred to as deployment.

When working with a digital agency, the agency will show you your website as development progresses. This is likely to be in a temporary hosting environment, and is unlikely to be using your final production domain name.

For example, your production domain name might be "bobsbusiness.com", but during the development period the website would be visible at the URL "agencyname.bobsbusiness.com". This is done to help you see what the website will look like and how it will behave before you take delivery, but without showing your unfinished website to the public.

Only when the agency has your agreement that the website is ready will the agency deploy the website. The act of deployment is to publish the finished website, moving it from its temporary hosting environment to its final production hosting environment where it is accessible by your customers.

The publishing of the website can be quite complicated and will include:

Copying source code files to the target hosting environment;

Creating the database for the website;

Configuring the host to use the production domain name;

Setting up automated backups;

Installing SSL to secure communication with the website;

Configuring payment gateways.

When working with a freelancer on a completely new website then the deployment stage maybe skipped by building the website directly in the final production hosting environment. This is a low-risk, money-saving solution that should be quite safe. Even if the unfinished website is live, few people will see your website until you start marketing it.

Training for you and your team

For anything other than a website of fixed, unmodifiable pages, there will be some aspects of the website that your business operations and sales teams needs to operate. For instance, you may have a business information website where the sales team has the ability to change the sales copy on the front pages; or if you have an e-commerce website then your operations team will need to keep production information up-to-date, and to pack and ship physical products when an order is received.

With the exception of a simple business information website, business users need to be trained to use the delivered solution before they can take over control of it themselves. The training may take many forms depending on the complexity of the delivery and how far away the two groups of people are.

Training examples include:

Delivering documents on how the website works;

An online demonstration by video conference;

Desk based training with a member of the web project team.

If we take the example of a content marketing solution, your external professional (e.g., freelancer, digital agency, etc.) will deliver you a blogging website, but the website will be empty. It is then up to you and your business team to start writing the articles that will populate the blog website and enable content marketing. Those same business users will need to be trained in how to enter their articles into the blogging website and how to correctly categorize them.

Technical support

However thorough the testing phase was, there is still a possibility that a website has problems when it is first used in production. There are many reasons for this—often it is just because your customers use your website in a slightly different way than you intended, thereby exposing unanticipated technical issues.

So that there is a shared understanding of the importance of these issues, it is useful to categorize them as follows:

Critical issues (or show stoppers);

Important issues;

Low priority issues.

On small projects you may communicate your issues by email with your external professional. However, on larger projects with bigger teams, and the potential for many more issues, there should be an issue tracking system in place. Every issue that arises should be entered into the tracking system, which then automatically notifies all the people that need to know.

Improve and iterate

Even if the website works exactly as designed, chances are that you will learn new things once the website is used publicly. Acting on this new information in a timely fashion might well be the only way for the website to achieve its business goals.

One example of this might be website performance. The functionality of the website might work exactly as expected, but more slowly than anticipated. The result may be that customers leave the website before completing the sales journey through the different pages you designed for them. Alleviating such performance issues may require more technical work and a redeployment into production.

Similarly, you may find that despite your best efforts, customers cannot easily navigate to the information you wanted them to find. Resolving this issue might require some quick changes to the website pages to improve the user experience.

Also, during the life of the website things may change (such as the number of customers using the service each day), and such changes may prompt further iterative improvements.

6. Can I do the web project myself?

What does it mean to do it yourself?

Having thought about the expense of hiring an external professional, you may be thinking at this point that you could do the work yourself and avoid a more costly investment. Keeping that thought in mind, let us look at the responsibilities associated with each phase of the project life-cycle to make it easier to see how much you actually might like to do yourself.

Define your website requirements

However much help and many ideas you get from other people, you should be defining the web requirements for your business. If you don't know where to start then you could either look at competitors websites yourself, or ask an external professional to propose key requirements that you could then approve or modify. However there would still be no escaping that the requirements must match your business strategy.

Business analysis

Nobody knows your business like you and your staff do. An external professional, no matter how technically savvy, will not be able to do any meaningful work until the analysis is complete. If your business team has experience documenting their business processes then they can write the business analysis themselves—there maybe one particular person on your staff to whom this job can be delegated. If you don't know what needs to be documented then another option is to let an external professional ask you questions and document the answers.

Ultimately, regardless of who does the business analysis, the small business owner will have the responsibility of approving it.

Designing the solution

On a small project where the technical solution is achieved using off-the-shelf software (e.g. WordPress), and the page design is a matter of choosing between a number of available pre-made templates, then the business owner can play the role of page designer by simply choosing the most suitable template. The business owner could also design the information architecture of the website by identifying which blocks of information should appear on each page.

A more custom project requiring custom web pages accordingly requires expertise in page design and graphical design (to define the fonts, colours, formatting, spacing and images for those pages).

Building the solution

There are "do it yourself" (DIY) website building tools (such as WIX), and there are WordPress themes aimed directly at business owners who want to build their own websites. If you opt for one of these solutions then you won't need a technical team. In my experience, these DIY solutions are only suitable for simple business information websites.

Apart from this "do it yourself" scenario you will need technical help to build the web solution. Technical help could range from hiring one freelancer to engaging a digital agency of some kind.

In the early days of the Internet, a number of business owners built their own websites. Typically these were business information websites that didn't have dynamic content and were not web applications. Furthermore, these websites didn't have the added requirement of being accessible on both desktop and mobile devices. Today the "do it yourself" website building tools are much better solutions than learning to write HTML web pages from scratch. However, anything more complicated than a business information website shouldn't be implemented using these solutions, because more complicated websites require dynamic content that can only be achieved through programming, which could take 2 years of study to gain a useful level of proficiency. The chapter on choosing the right technology goes into this subject in much more detail.

Testing

Whoever built the website will be responsible for initial testing. When this testing is complete then only the business owner and his team can conduct the user acceptance testing. With a small business, the business owner would be expected to take responsibility for signing off on achievement of the user acceptance testing goals.

Deployment to your hosting environment

If the website was built using a specialist website building tool (or a simplified WordPress installation) then the business owner and his team can themselves deploy the website to the production hosting environment. In any other scenario, knowledge of databases, servers, files and web servers is needed to safely achieve website deployment to the production hosting environment.

Training you and your team

If you built the website yourself and it has information that needs to be kept up to date, then you can train other members of your staff yourself on how to maintain the website content. If you did not build the website, then whoever did (e.g., freelancer, digital agency, etc.) needs to conduct the first training session.

Conclusion

From the review of roles and responsibilities for each phase of the project life-cycle it is clear that a business owner must be involved in making the key decisions. If he has a team then he can delegate some analysis, design and testing tasks to the team. Therefore there is no fully "hands off" approach to a project.

That said, it is difficult to see how a business owner can execute an entire project by himself. Only if the project is limited to creating a business information website on a website building tool would it seem efficient for the owner to do everything himself. Scenarios that involve building anything more complex will require web developers, and any completely original page design will require a web designer as well. The next chapter will expand on the roles of people who can help you.

7. Who can help me?

If you are not going to build a website entirely on your own then you will need to engage the expertise of other professionals.

What sort of experts will you need and what is the difference between them?

The experts that can help you with your website implementation include:

Web developer;

SEO expert;

Web designer;

Website project manager;

Web professional.

In the rest of this chapter, let us review the responsibilities of each of these roles so that you can decide which ones you may need for your project.

Web developer

The person who builds your website is called a web developer. This person's key skills are taking the design of a website (plus any business requirements and agreed user interactions) and delivering a fully working website. In a highly structured project the website design might be fully documented with a page by page graphical design, in which case the web developer needs to build pages which exactly match the design. This is a skilled role, which requires transferring every element of the graphical design to each web page. On the other end of the spectrum, in a less structured project the web developer might need to interpret the design from an email conversation and some rough sketches.

Building the part of the website visible to the public also requires knowledge of the differences between web browsers and how to make websites that work on mobile devices as well as desktops.

In addition to this, the web developer must build the processing that happens on the back-end of the website. For instance, any forms on the website need to be processed when they are submitted. A simple business information website may have very little back-end processing, but a custom e-commerce website would have a lot more. The web development skills needed to build the software needed for custom back-end processing are not the same as the skills needed to build web pages from detailed graphical designs; although you will find many people who have both skill sets.

There are many different website technologies ranging from website builder tools to CMS platforms (such as WordPress) to bespoke custom solutions. A web developer is not likely to be an expert in all of these technologies, therefore it is important to hire the right web developer for the right project. For instance a web developer skilled in building blog websites on WordPress may not be of much use building an e-commerce solution with Shopify.

Web designer

It is the web designer's role to propose how the website should look and how users should interact with it, and then to document all of this so that a web developer can implement the website.

A web designer may start by listening to your requirements, and then making rough sketches (e.g., wire-frames) of what each web page will look like. The web designer may then propose a colour scheme, fonts and logo (if you don't have one already) for the website.

The next stage would be to create a mock-up of each page in a graphical tool for review. Often these pages are created in tools such as Photoshop or Canva. The resulting page mock-ups should be as detailed as photos of the final web pages. It will be the web developer's responsibility to convert these page mock-ups into the HTML elements that are displayed in the browser.

Most websites are built to work on mobile devices as well as desktops. To address this the web designer needs to produce a design for each major size of screen (resolution) on which the website will be displayed. The web developer needs these different designs, because displaying a page on a small screen device is not just a question of shrinking the design down— instead the design of the page could radically change on smaller devices.

SEO expert

Designing your website so that it can be found easily in a Google search (or similar search engines) is termed Search Engine Optimisation (SEO). Ideally, how your website is going to be found by the search engines should be decided before the website is built.

The SEO expert may propose some changes that are visible to website visitors and some changes that are only visible to search engines. For instance, there may need to be visible changes where the SEO expert suggests that page title or page content lengths need to change. Alternatively, the SEO expert may suggest changes to the page source code that are readable by search engines but visually imperceptible to page visitors.

One of the critical responsibilities of the SEO expert will be to identify the keywords by which each page will be found by the internet search engines. This can be an involved process requiring a lot of input from the website owner and/or his marketing team to ensure that the website appears in the right categories and results for the right web search queries.

Once the keywords are identified for each page then they can be communicated to the web developer to be included into each page on the website.

Website project manager

The website project manager's responsibility is to coordinate the efforts of different people working on the project, to track their progress, to escalate any issues if necessary, to communicate their progress to the business owner and to ensure the website is delivered according to plan. In connection with these responsibilities, the project manager is likely to build a project plan that includes all the tasks that need to be executed, the dependencies between those tasks and assignments for who is responsible for each task. The original project plan is described as being the "baseline" of the project. Then as the project progresses the plan will be updated to reflect progress to-date, and new delivery dates may be calculated. The project resources in the plan should include both the people and the physical assets (such as the website hosting).

If you not wish to manage project resources yourself then it is a good idea to hire a website project manager. Ideally a website owner will only need to communicate with the project manager in order to be kept apprised of the project's progress and to give approvals when necessary.

Web security expert

You may also need a web security or internet security expert as part of the team. Depending on the project you might need a security expert all the way through the project, at key points (e.g. design and deployment) or you might manage without one altogether. If your business model has high security risks or you are doing something new then you are more likely to need a security expert. Alternatively if your technical solution follows a well trodden path then there may be industry best practices that you can follow without needing to engage a security expert; e.g. a simple e-commerce site can be built with WooCommerce, known trusted security plugins, secured with HTTPS on a managed hosting platform and that could be secure enough.

Web professional

By this stage you might be thinking that if each role is executed by a different person then your website will require a far bigger team than you had envisioned. If team size is a major concern then you may wish to engage a web professional.

A web professional aims to combine the roles of web developer, web designer, SEO expert and website project manager into one individual. The web professional would also have knowledge of web security. A web professional is ideal for smaller projects, as having just one individual handling the project reduces communication overhead and overall cost compared to having a team of people doing the same job. There is less advantage in using web professionals for larger projects that require more work than one individual can reasonably handle.

Of course, it is difficult for one individual to truly have the same expertise as a team of professionals who each have specific roles and expertise. Therefore, in practice the web professional must employ various strategies to ensure he delivers high-quality work; for example, using pre-made templates to reduce the need for a separate web designer, and off-the-shelf SEO tools to reduce the need for a separate SEO expert.

8. Choose the right domain name

What is the purpose of a domain name?

You need a domain name for your website. The address that you type into your browser to access a website is the domain name. For instance, Amazon's website has the domain "amazon.com". Every page within your website has this domain name at the beginning of its web address. The domain name consists of a name written in non-accented European characters, including any number of periods (full stops) followed by a domain name extension. Each country has a unique domain extension (for example .co.uk for the United Kingdom). There are also domain extensions that are considered global (for example .org).

Your domain name plays an important role in the success of your website. Customers will reach your website in one of these ways:

Typing the address directly into their browser;

Finding your website on a search website then following the link; or

Clicking a link from another website or email.

In the first scenario customers will only be able to find your website if they can remember the address, so it needs to be memorable and easy to type.

In the second scenario customers will only reach your website if the search engine they are using knows about your website and believes your website is relevant to a customer's search request. This is a big subject, but for now we can say that a domain name's inclusion of keywords is a significant factor affecting any search engine's decision on whether a website is relevant to a user's search.

In the third scenario the domain name can be hidden by the link text, in which case the domain name can have little to do with a customer's decision to click on the link.

The importance of branding

If you already have a successful business with a well-known brand name then your best choice for a domain name is likely to be your company name (or the trading name by which customers know your company). Once you have settled on this name you should choose the right root domain extension, and make sure the domain name passes the tests proposed later in this chapter.

Alternatively, if you are starting a new business or you have decided that you want your online business to have some brand separation from your existing business then you must put more thought into your choice of domain name.

The domain name of your website is an important part of your website's branding. You want visitors to remember the name of your website (i.e., the domain name), and associate it with the great products or services you are selling. When visitors think about your products and services you want them to remember your domain name and then visit your website to purchase those products and services. Unless you have a fantastically unique product or service offering then you are competing with many other websites to sell the same things. One of your key weapons in beating the competition and attracting customers to your website is the branding of your website, how it is perceived by your customers, and how it is reflected in your domain name.

Domain extensions

When the World Wide Web (WWW) first started there were very few domain names available and almost all websites seemed to have the .com extension. Since then the internet has grown exponentially and there are now many domain extensions that serve different purposes.

The most used domain extensions are:

.COM: 82.01 million

.DE (Germany): 13.05 million

.CN (China): 12.55 million

.NET: 12.42 million

.UK (United Kingdom): 7.83 million

.ORG: 7.79 million

.INFO: 5.24 million

.NL (Netherlands): 3.5 million

.EU (European Union): 2.98 million

.RU (Russia): 2.31 million

Source https://iwantmyname.com/blog/top-10-global-domain-extensions-statistics-numbers April 2018

Most of these are country-specific domain names, while others are used to indicate global websites. The ".COM" domain extension derives its name from the word commercial, and although it was originally intended to denote a United States website, in practice it is now used for any global business website. The ".ORG" domain extension is used to indicate a website owned by a global organisation (often a not-for-profit entity). The ".INFO" domain extension indicates that an associated website's main purpose is to provide information to visitors (therefore it is not generally used with e-commerce stores).

To help decide if you should have a global domain extension or a country-specific domain extension it may be helpful for you to consider the following questions:

Do you have a physical store/office that people will visit?

Is your product or service specific to a particular country?

Is your online business global with no physical stores?

If you answered yes to questions 1 and 2 then it would be good to use the country-specific domain extension of the country in which you are operating. For example, if you have a business selling Scottish Smoked Salmon across the world the business's website could benefit from having a global extension, but the business's brand is enhanced by people associating it with its home country so a ".UK" domain extension can also be a good option.

Alternatively, if you answered yes to question 3 then a global domain extension could be a better choice. The domain extension could be ".COM" or an extension that is even more specific to your business. For example, an online business with worldwide customers that sells market research reports might use the extension ".INFO".

If you are looking to create a website that is used globally and that is not strongly affiliated with any one specific country then you should use a global extension. The most used domain name extensions, excluding country specific domain extensions, are:

.COM

.NET

.ORG

.CO

There are many other global domain extensions including: ".BIZ", ".GOV", ".EDU" and ".IO".

Choosing your domain name

There is a continuing debate over how important it is that your domain name states what your business does. This is a difficult question because there are many good examples of businesses that are successful online with domain names that spell out what the businesses do, and also many good examples of businesses with domain names that seem to have no relationship to what the businesses do. However, we need to dig deeper because often these companies have strong brand names that they have invested heavily in so that we all know what their products and services are; e.g. the services company Accenture. Which works best? If you don't have a strong brand already (e.g. you are just starting out) then ideally your choice of domain name would be both good for brand building and also it would describe something about your website so that the website can be more easily found.

Good advice is to avoid long words in your domain name as these risk being misspelt. Keep the domain name short and use no more than three words. Avoid using numbers because some people will forget whether the numbers are typed as digits or words.

One way forward is to think of many alternative domain names. If you need ideas then write down the words that describe your business, then use a thesaurus to find alternative descriptive words and finally use these words on their own and then in combinations to make possible domain names. If you have access to an SEO expert then ask for a list of internet search keywords from your thesaurus list. With this list in hand, run the domain names through the following criteria and eliminate those that don't satisfy all three.

The following diagram summarises the tests to be considered when choosing a domain name.

Tests for choosing a domain	
1	Memorable
2	Easily typed
3	Easily pronounced
4	Not in use
5	Not too similar

First of all, make sure that the domain name is memorable. If it is impossible to remember then your website will never remain in the forefront of anyone's mind, and you will have difficulty attracting many new (or even repeat) visitors. Check that the domain name can easily be typed. Not everyone will find your website from a search engine, and many people will type your website name (e.g., perhaps the first time they visit). Eliminate the domain name if you find there is any difficulty in typing the name. Make sure that the domain name is easily pronounced. If you are going to have a large number of customers in other countries, think about how they might be able to pronounce your domain name. Verify that there is no ambiguity in how it is pronounced.

By this stage it is most important to confirm that the domain name is not already in use. You can do this by simply typing the domain name into the browser and seeing if any associated website is found. Alternatively, visit a domain registration website and use their search tools to see if your desired domain name is available for registration. If a domain name has already been registered then you should eliminate it from your list.

Last of all I would try to find the similarity of your domain name compared to existing names. This is a fuzzy search requirement because you won't know exactly which other domain names could be close to yours. My advice would be to type into the Google search bar the words that make up your desired domain name (each word separated by spaces), and see if any search results are websites with domain names so similar to the one you desire that customers are likely to be confused by the similarity. This is also the time to confirm that using your desired domain name would not infringe any third-party trademark rights—you should be able to find this out from the same Google search results.

Buying your domain name

When you have settled on a domain name you wish to use, and have confirmed that it is not being used by anyone else, then it is time to register it before anyone else does.

There are many domain name registrars available. These are the most used registrars:

GoDaddy

eNom

Tucows

HiChina

Network Solutions

1 & 1 INTERNET

PublicDomainRegistry

GMO Internet

Wild West Domains

Domain.com

Source https://www.domainstate.com/registrar-stats.html April 2018

To purchase a global domain name visit the website of a global registrar and follow the registrar's instructions. Normally the first thing the registrar will do is perform a domain name search to confirm that the domain name you wish to purchase is available. Alternatively, if you need a country specific domain name then it would be better to search on the internet for a registrar in that country, then go to that registrar's website and follow its instructions.

You will be asked to pay for the domain name before it is registered in your name. This normally only covers the cost of the domain for the first year. Expect that after approximately 11 months you will be invited to pay again for the domain name for the following year. If you fail to pay then the domain name very soon becomes available for someone else to purchase.

If you intend to use shared hosting then you may find that your hosting company offers a hosting package that includes a free domain name, in which case you can save some money by researching hosting options before registering your domain name.

Domain privacy

As part of the process of registering your domain name you will need to supply your business address, name and other contact details. The details you enter will then be available to the general public should anyone wish to see who owns your domain name.

If you don't want people to know you are the owner of the domain name, or you don't wish anyone to use this information for their own marketing purposes, then most domain registrars offer for purchase a service that will hide your true identity as the domain name owner. This service works by putting the registrars name and contact details on the public register rather than your own details.

It remains a personal choice as to whether having your name on the public register as the owner is an advantage or a disadvantage. Some people avoid domain privacy services simply because they are of the opinion that it is too risky to put a domain name (e.g., associated with an online business they have built up over years) in someone else's name.

Often when you purchase a new domain name you will receive official looking emails from third parties telling you that you need to pay for their domain services in the next 10 days to avoid a penalty or in order to complete your official domain registration. These are scams and should be ignored. Also, these are good examples of communications that would be avoided if you used a domain privacy service.

9. Should I use WordPress?

Small business website revolution

It is much easier and cheaper to build a good website today then it was in the early days of the Internet. The advancement in technologies and tools has been a revolution enabling lots of small businesses that wouldn't have dreamt of making money on the Internet to be successful. The primary driver behind this revolution has been "open source" software. Many web technologies are "open source" which in general means that they are free for most people to use with some specific restrictions depending on the open source model. Using these technologies businesses have avoided paying licence fees to technology suppliers and instead have only paid for the effort involved in building their website, sometimes even building the website themselves. Also many of these technologies are very efficient at building and maintaining websites. The biggest website open source success story is that of WordPress.

Why is WordPress often chosen?

There are lots of different web technologies and web platforms to choose from, so why have I singled out WordPress in this chapter? There are two main reasons:

Fact: more of the web is built on WordPress than any other platform;

Often even non-technical clients ask for a WordPress solution.

According to research from w3techs.comApril 2018, the WordPress platform powers more than 30% of all websites in the world. That is to say that more than 16 million websites are powered by WordPress. No other platform comes anywhere near this figure.

In my consulting work, when people ask me for a WordPress solution it is partly because of the popularity of the platform but more significantly it is because WordPress has a reputation for giving control to the website owner. People know that on a good WordPress website they will be able to update a lot of the content themselves, without bothering their technical support team. This was impossible in the early days of websites, when technical knowledge was needed to build and update every page.

WordPress is a very successful example of a Content Management System (CM).n The goal of a CMS is to make it easy for the content contributor to add new articles, create new pages, and add photos and videos quickly and easily; then to automatically display this new content with the chosen branding of your website (colours, fonts, logos, headers and footers).

WordPress is certainly not the only CMS for building websites, but it is by far the most used CMS in the World. Approximately 60% of all CMS websites are powered by WordPress.

What are people using WordPress for?

Typical uses of WordPress are:

Blog;

Business information website;

Personal portfolio website;

Public service websites;

Travel websites;

Photography websites;

E-commerce.

Three key reasons people choose WordPress:

Cost;

Easy customization using plugins and themes;

To maintain the website content themselves.

The core software of WordPress is open source, and as a result is available free for personal and commercial use. This can significantly reduce the cost of a web project compared to using other platforms. To create a complete website you may require customization in the form of WordPress plugins and WordPress themes. Tens of thousands of plugins and themes are also open source and free to use. If you need something even more specific then there are tens of thousands of plugins and themes that can be purchased for less than $100 each. Because there are so many WordPress websites, there are also a huge number of competent WordPress web developers who can help you build and maintain your WordPress website for a reasonable cost.

Evolving your use of WordPress

We know that there are many different online business models and, as a result, many websites are quite different from each other. We also know that WordPress is the most used website CMS platform in the world by far. However, WordPress is not always the best solution for every online business.

When discussing WordPress with my clients I often describe these 3 stages of evolution:

WordPress with "off-the-shelf" plugins and themes;

WordPress with some bespoke plugins and themes;

A completely bespoke solution.

I would estimate that the majority of the WordPress websites in use today fall into the first category. If your web project can be achieved with WordPress, off-the-shelf plugins, off-the-shelf themes and a WordPress professional to put it all together then you have a solid, relatively low-cost solution.

The next stage is one where your online presence requires a fresh or unique design that cannot be achieved with existing WordPress themes, or you require specific functionality that cannot be achieved with off-the-shelf plugins (e.g. a niche e-commerce solution). At this point you would need a WordPress expert to build a custom theme and/or plugin based on your requirements. This solution may still be your best option, as you still benefit from the flexibility of WordPress, but you are starting to move away from the WordPress mainstream.

The final stage is one where it is no longer a good choice to use WordPress. This is typically because the requirements have diverged so much from what can be done with "out of the box" WordPress that the total effort required to customize WordPress exceeds the effort required to build a custom solution without WordPress. The analysis of whether this is the case should also factor in long-term maintenance (i.e., a custom solution is likely to cost more to support than a WordPress solution, as WordPress provides maintenance updates for free).

8 reasons not to use WordPress

As popular as WordPress is, there are situations when using WordPress may not be the best solution. The previous chapter touched on one of these situations, which is where heavy customization is required. Here are 8 other reasons to consider not using WordPress:

When the number of website visitors is going to be very high;

When WordPress is not secure enough for the intended business use;

When page response speed is not fast enough with WordPress;

Lots of web page interaction is needed without refreshing the whole page;

When there is a high number of financial transactions each day;

If your audience's language is not supported well by WordPress;

When a high performance web application is needed;

When something simpler would be good enough.

WordPress was not designed to expect a huge number of visitors each day. If you have more than 10,000 visitors per day then it is worth considering a different solution. There are of course WordPress websites that have much larger numbers of visitors (e.g. New York Observer, New York Post and TED websites), but these have invested significantly to make WordPress a working solution for them.

One of the downsides of the popularity of WordPress is that it becomes an easy target for hacking attacks. This is not because core WordPress is necessarily any less secure than other platforms, but rather because hackers make great efforts to target WordPress knowing that a WordPress hack could give them the ability to exploit a huge number of websites. Also, not all plugins and themes have been written with the same quality as core WordPress, and using such plugins and themes could compromise the security of your WordPress website.

WordPress is a general purpose tool for building websites. That flexibility comes at the cost of page response speed. When adding a number of plugins and rich flexible themes the speed of delivering website pages to a browser can become noticeably slower. Similarly, some websites need to provide a very interactive experience without refreshing the page, which is difficult to achieve with WordPress.

Financial transactions can place quite a heavy burden on website performance, because they need to be guaranteed to succeed. This requires extra checks and controls in the software. The original design of WordPress never considered processing a high number of financial transactions. Doing so can lead to performance problems that hinder your ability to execute financial transactions with WordPress. For example, it would be difficult to use WordPress to run websites like PayPal.com or Amazon.com, which process enormous numbers of financial transactions each day.

WordPress is open source, which means it is developed and maintained by a community of people, most of whom are volunteers. They do the translation of WordPress menus, buttons and controls. As a result there have been cases where the quality of translation has been below what would be accepted in a commercial organization for a particular written language.

If the main purpose of your website is to deliver an online application to your users then WordPress may not be the right solution. WordPress excels in delivering pages of content to your users. If instead of pages of words and pictures you have only forms and controls (e.g., what in the past would have been built as a desktop application), then another technology platform maybe a better choice. An example of this would be online insurance quotation websites. Their purpose is not to display content about insurance (although there is some written content); rather, their real purpose is to have you enter your insurance requirements and calculate the quotation. The answer to each question determines the next question to be asked. Rarely is WordPress chosen as the platform for such an online web application.

Finally, there are times when WordPress is more complicated than necessary for the required solution. For example, if your business information website consists of only three pages that are not likely to change from one year to the next then a hand-written HTML solution may be good enough. This approach is being taken by the latest website generation tools, which provide tools to design your website and then deliver your website as a simple set of HTML files to be deployed on your web server.

10. The rise of website builders

What is a do-it-yourself website builder?

A "website builder" is an online tool used to create and host a simple website. The goal of a website builder is to allow a non-technical person to create and publish a website without needing help from anyone else.

Historically these tools were quite basic and they offered limited design choices. This situation has improved dramatically in the last few years, and a result the use of website builders has greatly increased. The latest website builders allow many design customisation possibilities, and even some have e-commerce facilities too.

Many small businesses start their online presence with social media, for example by creating a Facebook business page. The current website builders offer much more customization and control than the current social media single business page tools. Website builders can allow significant creativity over design and content. In particular, one of the greatest advantages of having your own website is that you can collect the names and contact details of people who are interested in your business, which you can later use for targeted marketing; in contrast social media platforms will not let you see the real contact details of the people who show interest in your social media business page.

However good social media tools are, a full business website conveys greater authority and fosters greater trust with customers. A website built using a website builder may be better than a social media business page, but it is likely to still lag behind a completely custom website or the latest WordPress themes (which have the advantage of being developed by different individuals and organizations). The website that looks the most professional is likely to be the one that has the greatest authority and builds the most trust.

The leading website builder tools let you see what the website will look like in the browser as you make your changes. This is distinct from the historical approach to building websites, which follows the cycle of writing code, saving the code, viewing the website, noting any modifications needed, returning to change the code, and repeating.

Website builders by market share

Market share of website builder tools globally:

Wix 23%

Squarespace 17%

Weebly 16%

GoCentral Website Builder 9%

Source http://www.statista.com/ April 2018

Wix is clearly the most widely used do-it-yourself website builder tool. However, putting this in perspective, only 0.6% of all websites globally used Wix, compared to 30% of all websites globally that are powered by WordPress.

Advantages of website builders

They are a great way to build a simple website yourself without needing any technical knowledge. Doing it yourself can reduce the cost of your website, with the added advantage that you can start work on your website as soon as you are ready—you need not spend time hiring a freelancer and communicating your vision.

Advantages of website builders include:

Cost;

Time to market;

Ready-made designs;

No technical knowledge needed.

If a business is on a tight budget then the cost of building a website with a website builder can be a huge advantage because no expensive professionals need to be hired.

Another big advantage is that you can make changes yourself any time you feel the need. This avoids delays spent waiting for your favourite freelancer to be available to work on your website.

Design templates are available with website builders to reduce your need to know how to create a good design, and also to save you time building your website.

No knowledge of hosting or deployment is needed with website builders. When the design is complete, the website can simply be published and is then available for the public to see. Websites are built by clicking or drag and drop actions.

Disadvantages of website builders

The main disadvantages of website builders are:

Very limited customisation;

Limited by your own experience;

Limited design templates;

Closed solution;

Changing design is difficult;

Limited scalability;

You never really own it.

Website builders can only ever offer a limited range of design customisation possibilities. If your business needs a unique design then you won't be able to get that with a website builder. Similarly, the latest design trends will not be available immediately with a website builder, whereas anything is possible with a completely custom website. A web professional can instantly identify a website made with a website builder, because of the limited designs.

One of the biggest disadvantages of building your first website yourself is that you don't have the benefit of experience, which a web professional would bring to your project (having probably built hundreds of websites already). This is true for all first time website builders, whether they use a website building tool or build a custom website.

Another disadvantage is that many people are not good designers. My personal opinion is that design sense is not something that greatly improves with experience—some people have graphical design skills and others don't. Not everyone knows what makes a good website; which elements to include and which to omit; how to make a website that looks good on a desktop and on a smart phone. Other website design considerations include ease of use, which is not intuitive without having some experience.

Each website builder tool has a limited set of design templates, and you cannot add your own templates. Compare this to an open source CMS such as WordPress, which has literally tens of thousands of design templates (themes) already available for free and many more available for a small cost (if no existing theme meets your needs, you can hire a WordPress expert to build a completely custom theme for you, as WordPress is open source and there are no restrictions on extending the platform).

The website builder tools with the highest market share are closed proprietary systems that cannot easily be extended. These same closed systems require a paid monthly subscription for continued use.

When changing the design of an existing website there is a risk that the website needs to be started all over again from scratch. In comparison, with a CMS it is usually possible to change the design template quite quickly (in order to see what another theme would look like) and then revert to the original template if desired.

Website builders also offer only limited scalability options. The technology of the website builder is aimed at building many small, low-volume websites. If your business was to grow, and the website struggled with the increased number of visitors every day, then there is little you can do with a website builder to improve the website's performance. Ultimately it would be necessary to build the website again using a higher performance web technology and on a higher capacity hosting platform. No high-volume websites run on website builder technology.

A website made using a website builder is never fully yours. Due to the proprietary technology used to build the website, there is no way to export the website and host it somewhere else.

Conclusion on website builders

A website builder can be a good choice if you want to build a website yourself, you want to start immediately, and you are not expecting a high volume of website visitors and you do not have the technical skills to build a website from scratch.

Even so, it would still be a good idea to consider building the website with WordPress and a good commercial theme instead.

11. How to choose the right technology

Efficient use of this chapter

This chapter aims to provide detailed information for each major online strategy. If you have already decided on your online strategy then you might only need to read the relevant sub-section in this chapter that explains how to choose the right technology for your particular strategy (and skip the sections that don't apply to you).

Static business information websites

There are a number of ways to build a business information website where the content doesn't change very often.

The following options can be considered:

Website building tool;

HTML website;

WordPress;

Website generator.

A "do it yourself" website building tool can be used to create your own business information website (see the chapter on website builders for more information). Any website with static content can be created by hand with HTML, unfortunately this process is time consuming and prone to errors. WordPress would be a heavy solution for such a light website requirement, but is such a cost effective solution with so many skilled freelance professionals available that it can nevertheless be a viable solution for static websites. Another, relatively newer, solution would be to use a website generator, such as Jekyll or Hugo, to create your static website.

Dynamic business information websites

The technical challenge with a dynamic website is much greater than with a static website. The dynamic website needs to display content that was not known when the website was built. This can be as simple as adding a new article or changing the main photo on a page.

The following options can be considered:

WordPress;

Joomla, Drupal;

Bespoke solution;

Do it yourself website building tools (limited cases).

WordPress, Joomla and Drupal are all Content Management Systems (CMS), and as such are being used all over the web for dynamic business information websites. These CMS platforms each make it very easy to add new pages and new posts once a website design has been established. WordPress has a much larger market share than Joomla or Drupal, and therefore more experienced freelancers and agencies are available to build WordPress solutions.

Often a large corporation opts for a completely bespoke solution for its dynamic business information website. This solution will not be cheap, but means that the corporation can get exactly the design that it wants built with technologies used across its organisation.

Some of the do it yourself website building tools can be used to build dynamic websites with some CMS functionality, although the customization options will be limited. If the business information website requires that any external information be included, this is perfectly possible with the first three proposed solutions, but not likely possible with the 4th solution.

Blog

A blog website is a special type of dynamic information website, wherein the dynamic nature is adding or modifying articles (the blog posts).

Global internet market share for blogging platforms:

WordPress: 20 Million websites

Google Blogger: 1 Million websites

Clearly WordPress is by far the most used platform for blogging. Bespoke custom solutions are barely used. Therefore if I was asked by a client to propose a blog website solution then I would only recommend WordPress, which is far more customizable. If you require a unique design for your blog then WordPress would also be a good choice.

E-commerce

There are many types of e-commerce. For this section let us consider e-commerce solutions for selling products online, for digital download or physical delivery. For example, this would include selling clothes (physical products) and e-books (digital products).

The following solutions are the market leaders and should be considered first.

Global e-commerce usage by market share:

WordPress with WooCommerce: 42%

Shopify: 7%

Magento: 4%

Source https://trends.builtwith.com/shop April 2018.

The WordPress core system has no e-commerce functionality. However, the very popular WooCommerce plugin integrates directly with WordPress and provides e-commerce functionality without any need for coding. WooCommerce has an entry level free tier, as well as a premium version and many paid add-ons to provide extra features (such as more advanced shipping rules).

Shopify is a hosted platform specifically for making e-commerce solutions. Therefore on the plus side it can be very quick to get going with Shopify, as no technical knowledge is needed and support is provided. The disadvantage, compared to WordPress with WooCommerce, is that you don't have full control over the solution, which could become a hindrance if you need to scale the solution or have a customized solution. Also, WordPress has far more designs available than Shopify, and more plugins for adding new functionality.

Magento is an open source e-commerce platform. Therefore it has more similarities with WordPress than it does with a hosted platform solution such as Shopify. Magento takes more time for a developer to set up, but has a much richer set of e-commerce features than standard WooCommerce. If you need a simple, low-volume e-commerce solution that can go live within a couple of weeks, then Shopify or WordPress might be better solutions than Magento.

High performance e-commerce

The market share for pre-built e-commerce platforms in the top 10,000 e-commerce websites in the world is quite different from the market share for standard e-commerce websites.

Platform market share for the top 10,000 e-commerce websites is as follows:

WordPress with WooCommerce: 10%

Magento: 7%

Shopify: 9%

Source https://trends.builtwith.com/shop April 2018

From the market share statistics above we can see that pre-built e-commerce platforms are used much less for the top 10,000 e-commerce websites in the world than for all e-commerce websites in the world. We can infer from this that the high performance e-commerce platforms are far less often built using WordPress. In fact, 57% of top 10,000 e-commerce websites don't use any of the market leading pre-built e-commerce platforms.

One reason is general pre-built platforms such as WordPress are limited in the volume of transactions they can process each day and the number of visitors they can support. Overcoming these limitations normally requires replacing the single box and single database solution with a distributed architecture spread across multiple physical servers, all of which requires a different technical solution.

In addition, when a business expects a high volume of transactions each day then it is normally at the stage where it cannot afford a disruption to its web service at all. The architecture needed for a high availability online solution is also a distributed architecture.

To achieve these high volume and high availability goals the least risky solution is a bespoke solution, where the builder has complete control over all aspects of the design and can build something exactly for the defined e-commerce requirements. This is no surprise when we think about huge e-commerce websites, such as Amazon.com, but many lower volume e-commerce websites, such as big name online grocery stores, also have their own bespoke solutions.

Note that Shopify and Magento have much higher market shares within the top 10,000 e-commerce websites in the world than they do across the whole internet.

E-booking

This is a specific type of e-commerce solution, which sells services or books rooms rather than delivering products. The challenge for e-booking is that the business model is significantly different from that of product selling e-commerce websites, and the same solutions that work for the latter will often not work for the former.

The following solutions can be considered:

WordPress with e-booking plugins;

Joomla and Drupal with booking add-ons;

Bespoke solutions.

WordPress, Joomla and Drupal with e-booking plugins are good solutions for websites with low to medium levels of online booking volume per day. If a high-volume booking website was needed then a bespoke solution would most likely be the best solution.

12. Choose the right payment gateway provider

Payment Automation

Typically the goal of e-commerce and e-booking solutions is to automate the sales process as much as possible, requiring as little manual intervention as possible (within your budget). As a result, you would normally want to process payment for your products and services online. There are many ways to do this.

Are online payments the right solution for your business?

Before you decide on the best payment gateway for your business, I suggest you consider whether online payment is the best approach for your business. As a rule of thumb, if your business requires frequent small payments then the overall cost of processing online payments will be insignificant compared to the overhead required by having manual intervention in your payment process. For example, with online grocery sales it is usual to only accept online payments.

In contrast, the online sale of high-value services is often transacted by bank electronic fund transfer or even by cheque. This is because such infrequent transactions don't require much manual intervention and the per transaction cost of most online payment gateways (approx. 3%) would significantly reduce profit margins on those sales.

The cost of online payments

To understand the differences between payment gateway providers, you will need to know the costs involved in using their services.

The different fees may include:

Account opening fee;

Platform fee;

Transaction variable cost;

Transaction fixed cost;

Account termination fee.

Some payment gateway providers will charge a fixed fee to open your account, and this account opening fee is normally non-refundable. A platform fee is typically charged every month, and is a fixed fee per month for having an account on a provider's platform that is assessed irrespective of whether any payments were processed or not. Transaction costs are fees for processing payment transactions. These fees can be a variable cost (where the provider may charge a percentage of the transaction as a fee for using the payment gateway to settle the transaction), or a fixed cost (where the provider charges a set amount (e.g. 1 dollar) regardless of how big the payment amount was). Some providers will also charge a combination of fixed and a variable fees on each transaction. When you have finished using a payment gateway and you wish to close your account then you may also have to pay the provider an account termination fee.

Online payment market share

The leading online payment gateway providers in order of market share are:

PayPal

Stripe

Square

ccBill

Despite these being global solutions, these gateways may not provide local currency services in every country. As a result, the market share of each of these market leaders may be much less in certain countries where a local solution is stronger.

Local currency payment maybe very important if you are providing a local online service, such as online grocery sales. Conversely, if you are selling global services to a global audience then you might do business in one currency only (e.g. only US dollars), and the availability of local currency payment would not be as important.

PayPal

PayPal operates in more than 200 markets and supports online payment in more than 25 currencies. It offers personal accounts and business accounts. At the time of writing it is far and away the market leader in online payments.

PayPal supports payments from consumer and merchant PayPal accounts, as well as receiving payments from credit and debit cards. In other words, when you accept payment on your website using PayPal then (most of the time) your customers have the option to enter their PayPal account details and pay using the funds in their PayPal accounts, or if they don't have a PayPal account then they can pay using a regular debit or credit card. In practice, PayPal wants all customers to sign up for an account with PayPal, rather than using their debit or credit cards. Therefore there are occasions when your customers will mysteriously not see the option to pay by debit or credit card.

Website integration with PayPal can take many forms. As a result of this flexibility it is fairly easy to start taking payments on a website using PayPal, which has no doubt been a major factor in the success of PayPal.

PayPal offers a range of different personal and merchant accounts to suit the activity of the account holder and the level of service required. The most basic account has no monthly fee, although the merchant accounts with higher service levels do have monthly fees.

Payment with PayPal on your website avoids Payment Card Industry (PCI) restrictions, because your customer is temporarily redirected to PayPal's website in order to complete payment. This means that no customer-specific card information is ever entered on your website. This can provide major advantages for a small business, including reduced costs in building online services and faster delivery of a working website.

Stripe

Stripe is a relatively new entrant to online payment processing, compared to PayPal. Despite this, Stripe already has a 17% market share and adoption of Stripe is growing fast.

To a website owner, one of the main differences between PayPal and Stripe is that Stripe does not hold any funds. There is no monetary balance on your Stripe account. Any payment made through Stripe is settled directly into the bank account of the Stripe account owner. As a result of this there is no concept of a Stripe-to-Stripe payment. Instead, all Stripe payments are from credit or debit cards into the regular bank account of the Stripe account holder. Therefore, in practice, Stripe is a credit and debit card payment processor. Despite the similarity with credit and debit card merchant acquiring systems, Stripe does not require a merchant account to be opened and does not charge a monthly account servicing fee (or any other monthly fee).

Payments with Stripe allow you to avoid PCI restrictions. Clever technology is used in the browser to avoid needing to store any card details, rather than redirecting the user to another website (like PayPal does), and in my opinion this provides a better user experience.

Once a Stripe account has been created, adding Stripe payment to a website is quite quick and does not require any inspection from Stripe itself.

High risk online payment

PayPal and Stripe have restrictions on which businesses can open accounts with them. The highest market share alternative payment processor is CCBill, which is a merchant account provider that specializes in high risk and international payment processing for e-commerce only businesses (not physical retail stores). CCBill provides payment facilities for online businesses that are not supported by many of the bigger processors, such as online dating websites and websites with adult content. These are considered high risk websites, and as a result the fees CCBill charges them for processing payments are understood to be higher than fees for lower risk online businesses.

Both credit and debit cards can be used to make payments through CCBill. Leading e-commerce solutions such as WooCommerce and Magento have existing integration features for CCBill.

Where to host your website

Big companies will already have their own data centres where they keep all their servers. When they put their businesses online they will host their websites in these data centres.

It is rarely economical for a small- to medium-size company to have its own data centres. Instead it is more effective to use third-party hosting companies that can reduce your costs by spreading data centre costs among many clients. This is achieved by hosting tens of thousands of websites from different clients at the same time. Without such economies of scale many small businesses would not have been able to start their online business.

There are different types of third-party hosting, each with different characteristics.

The main types of third-party hosting are summarised in the following diagram.

Website hosting choices

1. Economy Shared Web Hosting
2. Premium Shared Web Hosting
3. VPS (Bare Box)
4. VPS (Managed Server)
5. Dedicated Server

In the remainder of this chapter we will explore these different types of hosting.

Economy shared hosting

The lowest priced hosting solution is Economy Shared Web Hosting. This is also the most popular hosting used on the internet today. Despite this, it is unlikely to be used by any companies with a large web presence. On shared hosting your website shares the resources of a server with potentially hundreds or thousands of other hosting account holders. This has many implications. Most importantly it means that the performance of your website is not guaranteed because other hosting accounts may temporarily grab the resources that your website needs leading to degradation of performance. The biggest advantage of shared hosting is the cost savings achieved by sharing the server resources with other account holders; the second biggest advantage is that the server comes ready configured and supported by the hosting company. As a result, the lead time between opening your shared hosting account and publishing your website for everyone to see can be achieved in as little as an hour or two.

Another advantage of shared hosting is that usually the hosting package includes email. For example, having bought the shared hosting package you might be entitled to add 20 email accounts at no extra cost.

As you may expect, there are restrictions on the use of email with an economy shared web hosting package. Depending on the hosting provider you might find very strict rules on what constitutes spam (or junk) email. For example, I remember a situation with a major economy shared web hosting provider that rejected almost all the email confirmations coming from my client's e-commerce website, because the provider believed that the email subject used identified all the emails as spam!

Premium shared web hosting

Premium shared web hosting is similar to economy shared web hosting, with the main difference being that more resources are available to your premium shared hosting account. Typically that is achieved by sharing the same size server between less shared hosting accounts (e.g. maybe tens or hundreds of accounts instead of thousands). Your premium shared hosting account may also include higher thresholds at which it gets penalised for long periods of heavy use.

Because the server is shared between many hosting accounts there is little choice available for how the server is configured. For a general business information website this may not be a problem, but an e-commerce website with a growing number of visitors may require a particular configuration that would not be possible on shared hosting (premium or economy). Similarly, shared hosting will only support a very limited set of technologies. For example, all shared hosting will support WordPress, but if you needed to host an e-commerce solution that uses the Oracle database server technology (the number 1 commercial database platform) then this would not be possible with shared hosting.

Virtual Private Server (VPS)

When shared hosting is not enough for your website then the next major step up is a Virtual Private Server (VPS). With a VPS your website has guaranteed resources and at no point should the performance of your website be dragged down by the performance of websites on any other web hosting accounts. VPS is highly recommended for any business where your revenue or reputation is dependent on good website performance, especially for e-commerce solutions. Every business that I have worked with that started off on a low cost shared hosting platform migrated to a VPS within 2 years of successful operations.

You have complete control to install any software you desire on your VPS. Therefore if you had an e-commerce solution written in Java (the most widely used enterprise development software) with an Oracle database (the number 1 commercial database platform) then you could certainly run that on a VPS but you could not install it on shared hosting.

The downside is that a VPS is considered a professional solution by hosting companies, and therefore they don't expect to provide you with technical support. Typically the hosting company takes responsibility for the VPS being plugged-in and working, but does not support the software infrastructure needed to deliver the pages of the website, the databases etc. Furthermore, depending on the hosting provider, your VPS may only be accessible using the "command line" and you may not have access to graphical administration tools (such as cPanel or Plex). This can be a shock for a small business that managed to do everything themselves on shared hosting, and then after moving to a VPS is unable to use the server without regular access to a technical hosting expert. I have experienced this first-hand many times when the same hosting company that provided regular phone support for every issue on shared hosting suddenly refuses to help after transferring the website to its own, more expensive VPS, because support is no longer part of the hosting package.

One other difference between shared hosting and a VPS is that VPS does not include email. When you first get access to your VPS you will find that it is an almost empty box. If you want the VPS to host your email then you need to install and configure email software yourself. This needs to be considered when planning the upgrade and migration of a website from shared hosting to a VPS. Of course, there is an advantage to installing your own email software in that you will have full control over your email. You can set up your own spam filters, and there is no third party deciding what you can and cannot send, but it requires time and expertise. Alternatively, when upgrading to a VPS a better solution can be to subscribe to a professional email service such as Google Mail for Business, and avoid the responsibility of operating your own email server.

In conclusion, any successful e-commerce website that regularly faces performance issues on shared hosting should really consider moving to a VPS.

Managed VPS

If your company does not have the technical skills to support a VPS then one option that is available with some hosting providers is to pay extra for a "managed VPS". With this service the hosting company gives you access to their system administrators for a limited number of minutes or a limited number of issues per month. This option is considerably more expensive than a traditional VPS package, and if you are to take one of these services then I would strongly advise that you look carefully into the costs, including understanding how much support you get for free with your monthly contract and how much you would need to pay for after the free support limit has been reached.

Dedicated server

The ultimate hosting solution for high-capacity, high user volume and unlimited flexibility is a dedicated server. This has similarities with a VPS, except that you are given a complete physical server for your own use. With a VPS you are guaranteed certain server resources, but you still share the server with other VPS accounts so there is a physical limit to the resources available.

Like a VPS, a dedicated server would come as an almost empty box, and someone would need to install all the software and support it.

At the time of writing I have not been asked to migrate any websites from a VPS to a dedicated server. Therefore, in my opinion it is rare for a small business to need a dedicated server.

Shared hosting technical support

You will need to budget time and money to conducting the following activities on your shared hosting account, as the shared hosting company is unlikely to do them for you:

Deploying new versions of the website;

Installing new website software (e.g. upgrade WordPress);

Upgrading existing software (e.g. WordPress plugins);

Ensuring backups are working.

There is no reason for these tasks themselves to be particularly time consuming. Although the time needed to retest the website with new or upgraded software could be considerable. Many people on shared hosting simply deploy updates and upgrade their software with minimal testing. This is a risk you will have to assess based on your knowledge of your own business.

VPS technical support

When estimating the total effort and total cost of hosting a website on a VPS or dedicated server it is important to know that regular support is needed to manage the server. The time needed is considerably more than for shared hosting. Installing the server software and the website software is only the beginning.

Typical system administration support activities include:

Deploying new versions of the website and related software;

Installing mini-updates to plug security holes (patching);

Upgrading installed software to new versions;

Investigating errors that are reported by the server;

Looking for errors in log files that might be an indication of future problems;

Tuning the database server as volumes increase;

Tuning the server as visitor volumes increase;

Re-installing software after hacking attacks.

These would be described as system administration or system operations tasks. They require specialist system administration skills, which are quite distinct from website development skills.

In addition to these tasks the web developer would need to make updates to the website and test updates to the website.

Hosting market leaders

The leading hosting providers globally are:

GoDaddy

1&1

Amazon Web Services (AWS)

Strato (Germany)

OVH (France)

Hetzner Online (Germany)

Blue Host

The market is quite fragmented, with the biggest global hosting company (GoDaddy) having less than 5% market share.

All of these 7 market leaders offer both shared hosting and VPS. Economy shared hosting can be found for less than $10/month. Expect to pay double that amount for premium shared hosting. Bare VPS hosting (only recommended for experts) is available from $10/month. Although most people would find managed VPS hosting less time consuming, and it starts at around $30/month (with a powerful server more likely $50/month). If you need extra support for your web hosting (outside the existing contract budget) then expect to pay at least $50/hour.

The market leaders also include Amazon Web Services (AWS), which is far from being an economy hosting solution for small businesses. Many AWS clients have professional bespoke web solutions, and could well be paying hundreds of dollars per month for their high-capacity hosting.

WordPress managed hosting

Every website platform has its own specific support requirements, in addition to general server support. With the popularity of WordPress a number of WordPress-specific hosting solutions have become available. These provide a premium service aimed at professional WordPress users, typically with a high number of regular website visitors, who don't want to get involved in the details of WordPress technologies too much.

In 2018 the leading dedicated WordPress managed hosting providers include:

WP Engine

Siteground

Flywheel

13. Can all your customers use your website?

The World Wide Web (WWW) is built on open standards. This means that anyone who wishes can read the standards and build their own internet browser. As a result, not all of your customers are likely to be using the same type of internet browser. Unfortunately, because each software company has interpreted the WWW standards slightly differently, the browsers they built each work slightly differently. Additionally, the WWW standards constantly evolve, and browser companies need time to catch up. At any point in time the various browsers will have different features from each other.

The main browsers on the desktop by market share are:

Chrome: 60%

Internet Explorer: 12%

Firefox: 12%

Edge: 4%

Safari: 4%

Source https://netmarketshare.com/browser-market-share.aspx April 2018

Therefore, any website built for a general audience needs to work with at least these top 4 browsers.

To add to the differences between the browsers, the internet open standards have evolved over time and the browser companies need time to catch up. Therefore at any point in time the browsers will have different features to each other.

When testing you need to make sure that your whole website is tested on at least the most common browsers used by your target customer group. Then you need to make a business decision on how much more time to spend testing (and potentially fixing problems) with your website on less used browsers that you know some of your customers will use.

Internet browsers on smart phones also behave differently compared to their desktop equivalents. This is true even for the same model of browser. For example, Safari on an iPhone does not behave exactly the same as Safari on the desktop.

These are the most used browsers on smart phones:

Chrome: 62%

Safari: 28%

UC Browser: 3%

Opera Mini: 3%

Android Browser: 2%

Source https://netmarketshare.com/browser-market-share.aspx April 2018

Therefore you can appreciate that building a website that works with every possible internet browser used by every possible customer can be a daunting task. A vanilla WordPress solution or a "do it yourself" commercial website builder tool should already work with multiple browsers thanks to efforts made by the platform developers. However, as soon as you add your own customizations and third-party plugins then testing with different browsers is as important as if you had built an entirely bespoke solution.

Similarly, as part of your digital strategy you will need to estimate the percentage of your target customers that will use smart phones and other mobile devices. You will then need to test your website with the browsers that your target customers will use on these devices.

14. How to connect with your online customers

How can your prospects ask questions?

Visitors to your website may not find all the information they need by reading your pages. The information they need could be on your website, but the visitors just can't find it; or the answer to their question may simply be missing. In this situation you risk losing visitors before they become customers. If they don't find what they want then they are likely to simply leave your website and look for another that does offer them what they want.

To avoid this problem it is necessary for your website to offer one or more methods that the customer can use to ask you a question.

Contact us

The simplest approach to facilitate communication with your customers is to implement a "contact us" page on your website. This page has a form where the visitor can enter their contact details and whatever message they wish to send (usually a question).

In recent years these "contact us" forms have been exploited by robots that use the form to automatically send spam to website owners. To avoid this it is a good idea to have an additional question that can only be answered by a real person. These can be quite sophisticated questions such as entering the answer to a mathematical sum, or using a Captcha widget that requires entering numbers and letters from a displayed photo.

Website live chat

An improvement over the "contact us" page is offering a dynamic website chat feature on your website. As soon as a visitor clicks on the chat icon they can start a real live conversation with the website operations staff. The operations staff will receive an alert that a request for a chat has been received. Whichever staff member is free can then accept the chat and start to communicate with the visitor.

A number of studies have reported that many customers need to be able to get instant help when buying online, and website live chat is a good solution for that.

My personal experience is that I have had a lot more engagement with potential customers once I added a chat tool to my website.

Issue ticketing platforms

For online service businesses, customers will want to report problems that need to be tracked and investigated. To avoid customer issues being lost in a sea of other content reported by email, a more professional solution is to use an issue ticketing platform. This differs from email in that each issue is assigned a ticket number and there are normally some questions to be asked that help direct the customer issue to the right team (e.g., is this is a technical problem or is it a billing problem). Issue ticketing platforms also streamline the work of the internal teams dealing with the customer issues, making it easy for teams to see which issues are open, which are urgent and how many there are for a particular category.

In 2017 the leading online issue ticketing platforms included:

Zendesk;

Intercom;

Help Scout;

osTicket;

LiveAgent.

Of course, not every website will require an issue ticketing platform. It depends on how many service issues your customers raise on a regular basis. Also, on a major e-commerce website this functionality might be better achieved as a custom solution within the website, rather than using a third-party ticketing tool (this is common approach with many high-volume, market-leading websites).

15. Regulations that can't be ignored

Are there any online regulations?

You may be thinking at this stage that the internet is a fresh and new place, where old world restrictions on business don't apply. Unfortunately, not only do the old business laws apply, but there are also new regulations just for the online world. In addition, if your online business operates in many different countries then you need to consider regulations in each of these countries.

The purpose of this chapter is to give you an overview of the different regulations, laws, directives and rules with which your business may need to comply in order to implement your digital strategy. The author is not a lawyer, and this chapter is not a substitute for professional legal advice.

Identification

In many countries it is a requirement set in law that the legal name of a business is displayed clearly on the business's website and on any correspondence sent by that website. The full registered address and any company registration number should be visible on at least one easily accessible page of the website. If your business has them then you may also have to display your sales tax registration number and data protection number on the same page as the address.

An example of this law is the United Kingdom Companies (Trading Disclosures) Regulations 2008.

Data protection and privacy

Laws exist in many countries to protect information from visitors to your website, and information collected about your customers online. The common thread of these laws is prohibiting the misuse and the unauthorized sharing of this information with third parties.

Such laws include:

Singapore personal data protection act 2015;

United Kingdom Data Protection Act 1998;

United States Data Protection Act 1998;

Australian Privacy Act;

New Zealand Privacy Act 1993;

Personal Information Protection and Electronic Documents Act (PIPEDA);

European Union GDPR.

In the European Union the law even includes regulation of the tracking information in "cookies" created by your browser.

As a result, the best solution is to avoid storing visitor information that you don't really need. The less visitor information you have the less problems you create for yourself and your business. If you do store any visitor information then you immediately become responsible for keeping that user data private. This may require encrypting user data so that it is unreadable by others, controlling physical access to the servers on which user data is stored and doing everything possible to maintain a strong level of internet security to stop user data from being stolen by hackers.

PCI DSS

This is a set of security standards issued by the Payment Card Industry (PCI) Standards Council to ensure that debit and credit card information remains secure. These standards are known as the Payment Card Industry Data Security Standards (PCI DSS). The standards apply to any organization that accepts, stores or transmits card data. Therefore it applies to the online processing of card data as well as physical card swiping and payment by phone. Failure to comply can result in termination of card processing agreements or a monetary fine or both.

Multiple levels of compliance exist. Each major card processor has different criteria for determining which level an organization needs to comply with. Therefore the first step to ensuring compliance is to visit the card processor websites for each of the card types you wish to process, and to read the processors' instructions on how to determine which level of compliance you need to achieve.

The most significant element in achieving PCI compliance is whether the mechanism your website uses for online payments results in payment card details ever being stored on your website. Some online payment solutions avoid storing card details; these include the two online payment market leaders: PayPal and Stripe. Unfortunately, using online payment solutions from many other major payment providers would result in your website temporarily (or permanently) storing card data.

If your payment solution does store card data then to achieve compliance special attention must be paid to:

Having a secure online network;

Protecting card data;

Executing a vulnerability management programme;

Monitoring access to card data;

Implementing and maintaining a policy for information security.

The network in which the servers that store card data exist must be securely separated from the rest of the world with a good firewall, and using best practices to create a private network. This can be problematic with shared hosting, because even though the hosting provider will use a firewall to control server access from the outside world, there is still a risk that other shared hosting users could gain access. If you need a PCI DSS compliant environment for your hosting then it would be advisable for you to confirm this with any potential hosting providers before entering into a contract with them.

Card holder data needs to be protected using industry best practices, including strong user password security policies, and physically restricting access to data centres and server cabinets. All data must be encrypted before transmission.

There must be a vulnerability management programme in place that includes anti-virus scanning, regular updating of security patches and subscribing to security breach alerts. It is necessary to keep track of all access to stored card data, and be able to audit user access. An information security policy needs to exist, and to be actively used and maintained. This will include regular security risk assessments and operational security procedures.

Depending on the required level of compliance it may also be necessary to conduct an authorized security scan. This must be executed by a PCI Authorized Scanning Vendor. The results from the scan must be submitted to your acquiring bank together with a Security Access Questionnaire.

European General Data Protection Regulation (GDPR)

This European Union regulation effective from May 25, 2018 aims to give back control to European Union users of online services. It replaces the European Data Protection Directive of 1995.

In summary, businesses offering services to EU citizens online need to provide the following:

Clear statement of who they are doing business with;

Agreement from the customer that their data can be collected;

Explanation of why data is being collected;

State what the collected data will be used for;

Who will receive the data that has been collected;

Ability for the customer to access their data;

Export of each customer's own data;

Allow customers to delete their data;

Deliver a report of the customers data within 40 days;

Inform customers if any breach of data security occurs.

Breaches of data privacy policy by the website owner, or any party with which that data is shared, must be communicated to all website customers affected within 72 hours of the website owner being aware of the breach.

Many websites already collect data in many ways. For the purposes of GDPR all of the following are deemed personal data collection:

Registration of new users;

Newsletter sign-up;

Blog post comments;

Website visitor traffic logging;

Logging from website security tools;

Website visitor analytics;

Contact page message submissions.

One way to achieve compliance is to avoid storing too much personal data. For instance, contact forms can simply forward form data by email, and not store that data in the website's database. When it is impossible to avoid data storage then the full mechanisms described above need to be implemented.

Failure to comply with GDPR risks incurring EU fines up to the greater of EUR 20 Million or equal to 4% of annual turnover!

Consumer protection

When building an e-commerce website that includes quoting product prices (even if there is no physical delivery from the website) then consumer protection laws must be adhered to.

Examples of these laws are:

UK Consumer Protection (Distance Selling) Regulations;

Electronic Commerce Regulations (EC Directive).

The following areas of your online business must comply with these laws:

Shipping and delivery policy;

Refunds policy;

Terms and conditions.

The shipping and delivery policy of your online business needs to be clearly displayed on your website. This can also include stating what your business is not liable for.

In many jurisdictions there is a legal requirement to give customers a cooling off period during which they can cancel their purchases and request a refund without any questions being asked. The length of the cooling off period depends on the country your business is operating from/in. Your business's policy for refunds must be clearly displayed on your website. In that policy you need to be clear about whether there are any fees to be paid for the refund; e.g. a re-stocking, admin cost or shipping cost for the return of physical goods.

The terms and conditions on your website can include all the conditions above. It also needs to state that the purchase of any goods on the website forms a contract between the customer and the supplier (your online business legal entity).

Therefore, the following clauses should be included in your terms and conditions:

Business identification;

Which legal jurisdiction is being used;

Shipping and delivery terms;

Refunds policy;

Limitations to your liability;

Data protection;

Protection of intellectual property and trademarks;

Website terms of use.

Your terms and conditions need to state under the laws of which country the sales contract is being made.

Accessibility and discrimination

Many countries have specific laws, guidelines and directives to ensure that disabled people are not discriminated against. In some countries these laws extend to ensuring the accessibility of websites to disabled people, such as individuals with limited eyesight.

Examples of these laws are:

The United Kingdom Disability Discrimination Act 1995;

Americans with Disabilities Act 1990;

EU Directive 2016/2102 (public bodies).

Often these directives are much stronger for public bodies than for purely commercial organizations. This is particularly noteworthy for government agencies and educational establishments that wish to be online.

In practice, action will need to be taken if your website has:

Photo images;

Audio messages;

Images with text.

Every image that is displayed on your website needs to have an alternative descriptive attribute, so that a person with limited vision accessing your website with an automated screen reader will still understand what the website is for and how to use it.

Audio messages on your website should be accompanied with equivalent textual captions to assist people who are hard of hearing.

If the website has images with significant textual content that cannot be interpreted by a blind person's screen reader then a text caption alternative should be made available.

Anti-spam laws

In general, spam comprises unsolicited messages sent in bulk for commercial purposes (e.g. an email advertisement). The message is unsolicited if the recipient has never agreed to receive commercial messages in this way from the sender. If a customer wants to unsubscribe from your mailing list and you continue to send them commercial advertising messages then that becomes spam.

Anti-spam laws include:

United States CAN-SPAM Act;

Australian Spam Act 2003;

Canada Anti-Spam Law (CASL) 2014;

New Zealand Unsolicited Electronic Messages Act 2007.

Collecting taxes

Your online business may be legally obliged to collect taxes by the legal jurisdiction in which the business operates. Furthermore, there may be local assumptions about displaying prices with or without taxes that you may want to follow to avoid any surprises for your customers.

The tax you are most likely to need to consider is sales tax, in some form or another. Taxes may be defined by the country in which you are operating, and perhaps also by the state in which you are operating. Often sales tax applies to certain goods and not others. There may be special taxes, such as green taxes, to be applied to goods that have a high cost to recycle.

If you have a new company, or one with a yearly revenue below a certain threshold, then in some jurisdictions you may be exempt from collecting sales taxes.

Copyrights, trademarks and patents

Trademarks are unique ways in which your business is identified. This can apply to business names or symbols. Only when you have a trademark can your business be protected from another business copying your brand identity. A trademark is only valid in the legal jurisdiction in which it is registered although in some jurisdictions common law trademark rights can provide protection for unregistered trademarks. In the United States a trademark can be registered for a particular state and/or country wide.

A freedom-to-operate analysis (FTO) is a good place to start if there is any doubt about infringing any patents by putting up your website and selling your planned products or services. This involves searching patent literature and seeking a professional opinion as to whether any existing patents will be infringed.

If you have a unique symbol or name but you don't intend to register your trademark in the short term then it is advisable to put "TM" in superscript next to your trademark on your website to declare to everyone that you consider the symbol or name to be your trademark. In case of a dispute this should help to provide some historical proof that you have been using the trademark, and may prove that your business was the first to use it.

Patents protect the holder from having other people copy their inventions. Even if your online business does not need to register patents, you would still want to be sure that you are not infringing anyone else's patents.

Copyright protects works of art, music and textual content. On your website it would be wise to state what is protected by copyright. Also you will want to be sure that nothing on your website infringes anyone else's copyright. Note that it is easy for a web developer to unwittingly include a copyrighted photo or icon that he has found on the internet and then to forget to replace it with a new image before the website is made public.

Protection of minors

Unlike a physical store, on your website you can't physically see who comes to your website or how old they are. In many countries there are laws protecting the collection of information from minors and also restricting the sale of certain products to minors.

Relevant laws that need to be complied with include:

United States Children's Online Privacy Protection Act (COPPA);

European GDPR.

Under both of these laws a website must obtain consent before data related to children under the age of 16 can be collected.

In most countries there are also restrictions on the sale of certain products to minors, including:

Fireworks;

Aerosol paint;

Alcohol;

Weapons and firearms;

Strong glue;

Tobacco;

Video recordings (of adult classification);

Video games (of adult classification).

If you have an e-commerce website selling any of these products then you will need to take all reasonable steps to stop minors from purchasing these products. This can be achieved by including the restrictions in your website's terms of use, placing prominent information about the restrictions on the same page as the products, having an age-checking pop-up and having the customer tick a box to confirm that they are an adult before completing a sale on the checkout page.

Advertising and marketing

Most countries have laws to protect consumers when subject to advertising and marketing. These laws include:

US Federal Trade Commission Act (FTC Act);

UK Consumer Rights Act 2015.

To be in compliance with these laws, all marketing and advertising online (websites and emails) must be:

Honest;

Legal;

Decent;

Truthful;

Socially responsible.

In this context "socially responsible" means that the advert should not cause harm or offence. Furthermore the adverts should not be aimed at causing social unrest.

Particular care needs to be taken when using the word "free" in an advert. To use this word the product or service must really be completely free without any hidden fees (e.g. shipping costs or membership).

There are also specific additional restrictions on certain products being advertised. This often includes the following products:

Alcohol;

Medicines;

Tobacco;

Food;

Beauty products;

Environmentally-friendly products.

One of the main themes in these laws is that advertising and marketing must not deceive the customer in any way. This encompasses both deception by including false information and deception by deliberately leaving out certain information. The laws also aim to protect the consumer from aggressive sales techniques.

The country in which the advertising is taking place may also have specific advertising restrictions on:

Gambling;

Advertising to minors;

Political advertising.

In addition, there are specific regulations protecting other businesses. It is illegal to use a competitors' logo or name in an advert such that it would mislead the consumer as to the true identity of the advertiser. Also it is illegal to make comparisons with a competitor's product when it is not the same type of product as yours, as this would be an unfair comparison.

If you have any doubt about the marketing or adverts that you want to publish then you should seek professional legal assistance for the jurisdiction(s) in which you are operating.

People's Republic of China

There are specific regulations regarding the operation of a website in the People's Republic of China that may not be obvious to people outside the country.

To operate a website in China first requires the purchase of a Chinese top level domain name (a domain name ending in ".cn") from one of the few domain registrars that are approved by the Chinese Ministry of Industry and Information (MIIT). Then the website itself needs to be registered with the MIIT. When applying to register the website with the MIIT the applicant must already have a registered business licence for operating in China and the person applying must have proof of being a citizen of the People's Republic of China.

China's cyber-security law is similar to the European Union GDPR, but with additional restrictions.

Any company operating Critical Information Infrastructure must keep customer data within China. In order to send any customer information overseas it will be necessary to obtain consent from the Chinese government. This is referred to as "data localisation".

16. Is your website secure?

Very real security risks

Your website is at risk of malicious attacks. The internet is a wild place with both criminals and hobbyist hackers waiting to take advantage of the unwary. At any time you risk being faced with any one of the following problems:

Your customers are unable to access your website due to a DoS attack;

Your website is displaying someone else's adverts because it was hacked;

Unauthorized links to third-party websites appear;

Your login account no longer has the rights to update your website;

Parts of you website behave strangely because they have been infected;

Customer personal data is stolen from your website;/or

Your payment credentials are used for unauthorized purchases.

What is the goal of these malicious hackers?

The motivation for hacking websites varies. Malicious hackers' main goals usually fall into the following categories:

Monetary gain;

Stealing private information for sale;

Using private information for identity theft;

Sending spam;

Free advertising;

The technical challenge.

The first step of an attack is gaining complete control over your website. Then once they can modify your pages, send emails as you and install their own software the hackers are ready to pursue the real goals of their attack.

There is no one single reason for malicious attacks. The good news is that there are measures that you can take to avoid these problems and to recover from them if they occur.

First, we need to explore what the different attacks are and how they take place.

Attacks are often not human

To better understand the threat to your website security it is useful to understand who attacks websites. Attacking websites has evolved significantly from when/how lone hackers were first portrayed in films.

These are the different attackers that your website may face:

Human hackers;

A single robot hacker (bot);

Network of robot hackers (botnet).

Modern hackers are likely to be well-connected online, and will often communicate with other hackers. Through the internet they may share information and tools to make their hacking more efficient. They share vulnerabilities for a particular website software and version. Once the hacker knows the software running your website then he can consult online documents and forums for clues on how best to attack your website.

The attackers themselves are unlikely to get tired when they use a robotic device (called a "bot") to do the hacking for them. This is how they can execute an attack that lasts for days, trying all sorts of different ways to gain access to your website.

Many of these bots can be run at the same time, thus creating a network of robot attackers. This network is described as a "botnet".

The use of bots is so widespread that you are much more likely to have your website attacked by a bot than by a real person. There is an advantage to this because a human attacker can be very resourceful in how they attack whereas a bot will be limited to some simple hacking tasks for which it was created.

Login attacks

This is often described as a "brute force attack" and is most often implemented through a bot. The bot has a long list of possible user names and passwords, which it tries one after another until it manages to gain access to a target website. The user names and passwords may be from a list of likely passwords for all internet websites, and then the bot may apply some random variations.

Remember that this type of attack can be directed at any part of your website infrastructure that uses login names and passwords. For example, the web-server has a login and so does any CMS (such as WordPress) that you are using. Also, your website itself may have a member or customer login page that is vulnerable to this type of attack.

Software vulnerabilities

Any software that is used to either build your website or host your website could have known weak spots that hackers can exploit. When a hacker inspects your website prior to an attack he will be looking to identify which types of software you are using and which versions are installed. With this information he can plan which attacks he is going to make.

One of the most common software vulnerability attacks is an SQL injection attack. This is usually an attack aimed at data entry forms on a website. The attacker crafts values for the website form fields that when received by the server allows the attacker to run malicious queries on the database. Good web development practices can greatly reduce the risk of this type of attack.

Software manufacturers will eventually become aware of the vulnerabilities in their software, will fix these vulnerabilities and release new versions of the software. Therefore one of the easiest ways to avoid being hacked is to keep all software up to date.

Shared hosting attacks

This type of attack applies to any environment where multiple services are running on the same server (e.g. an economy shared web hosting platform). It is possible that a hacker will find the most vulnerable website, take control of it then use that website's privileges to attack other websites on the same server. This is less likely to happen with shared hosting providers that take your website security seriously and invest in measures to avoid these problems, but the risk is still present with a large number of shared hosting providers.

VPS and dedicated servers are less likely to suffer from this problem, especially if you take a serious attitude towards web security and keep everything up to date.

Denial of service attacks

The intention of a Denial of Service (DoS) attack is to stop a website from providing a service to its real users. This is achieved by flooding the website with requests pretending to be from real people. For example, a website may have been built to service 10,000 visitors in one day, but the DoS attack sends 10,000 new visitors every 10 seconds to the website. Often under this amount of unplanned load the web-server will crash because it runs out of resources before it can respond to all the requests it receives.

Identifying a DoS attack usually relies on filtering real visitors from attacking visitors. Often this assumes that the attacking visitors all have something in common, for example they may come from the same internet address. With the attacking address identified any further connection requests can be blocked.

A more aggressive version of a DoS attack is a Distributed Denial of Service (DDoS) attack. These are far less common and more difficult to identify. A DDoS attack is effectively a DoS attack executed from many different locations in the world simultaneously. As DDoS attacks come from completely different internet addresses they are much harder to detect and resolve.

What can you do to improve security?

There are many ways to reduce the risk of your business being compromised through an online attack. These include:

Build for security;

Restrict privileged accounts;

Keep software up to date;

Hosting choices;

Third-party security solutions;

Website penetration testing.

Most important of all is to build your online services in such a way that attacks are unlikely to succeed. A good web developer should take measures to reduce attacks to the website they are building. This is especially true for SQL injection attacks which are difficult to resolve if poor design decisions were made in the beginning.

Malicious hackers can only cause damage when they have access to privileged accounts that have the rights to make changes on your hosting. To avoid brute force login attacks it is best to have as few accounts as possible that having full administration privileges. Those accounts that do have administration privileges should have very strong passwords that are difficult to guess.

Hackers can easily target known weaknesses in known software packages. Once simple way to protect against this is to upgrade your website software as soon as a new version is released. The new version will have fixed the security weaknesses in the previous version. Using old software with well-known weaknesses is very risky.

Shared hosting attacks can't happen if you don't choose to use shared hosting or you pick a shared hosting provider that stakes its reputation on such attacks not happening. Despite this, if you have a small budget then it might be better to rely on the web security provided by shared hosting rather than to have a VPS with no security measures at all.

Because website security is such an important issue you will find that there are a many third parties that offer software solutions to reduce your online risk. Some have free plans for small business and low-volume websites. For example, if you are using WordPress then there are plugins, such as Defiant WordFence or iThemes Security Pro, that are very effective against attacks.

Even if you have all these security measures in place then you still won't know how secure your website is until someone tries to break in. If you have the budget you may wish to pre-empt this black day by paying an internet security company to try to break into your website in order to identify, and then plug, any holes in your security. This is known as website penetration testing, and it is often conducted by "white hat hackers", who may themselves have once been malicious hackers (black hat hackers).

17. Your digital marketing strategy

The World Wide Web is enormous. There are at least 1.7 billion websites. However, internet visitors are not equally distributed between all these websites—some websites are extremely popular while others get almost no visitors at all. Less than 1 million websites receive more than 50% of all visitors. Clearly not all websites were made equal.

Therefore it is critical to avoid the mistake of believing that putting your shiny new website on the Internet will be enough for people to find it and start using it.

Over the years this has been a regular theme at the start-up Meetup group that I host. Frequently, people attending the meeting have built great products, but their work is not being noticed and as a result they are not acquiring customers.

To achieve success it is important that you have a "Digital Marketing Strategy" to improve the discover-ability of your online business. As part of your strategy you will also need an "SEO strategy" to improve how search engines (e.g. Google) help customers find your website.

There are multiple ways that people may find your website and ultimately become customers. In digital marketing each of these categories is called a marketing channel. Depending on your existing or intended business model you may use one or more of these marketing channels:

Organic search

Content marketing

Email marketing

Social media marketing

Search engine advertising

Mobile marketing

Online paid adverts

Webinars and virtual events

We will now explore these channels in more detail.

Organic search and SEO

The process of using a search engine (such as Google) to find websites is called organic search. It is organic because it is the true result of the search engine, without influence from paid search results. There are multiple search engines that your potential customers could use to find your website.

The leading global search engines by market share are:

Google: 91%

Bing: 3%

Yahoo: 2%

Baidu: 1.5%

Source http://gs.statcounter.com/search-engine-market-share April 2018

As you can see, Google is by far the most important search engine, and you will want to be sure that your website appears in Google's search results. That said, it is still worth trying to appear in the search results of the remaining leading search engines. The good news is that the mechanism that Google uses to read the information from a website is also used by the other search engines, so there is no reason not to be searchable by all the major search engines.

Improving how your website appears in the ranking of results from the search engines is called Search Engine Optimization (SEO). The algorithms used by search engines are both complex and secret in their details. Despite this, we know that the two main features over which we do have control are:

Content

Domain authority

Roughly speaking the words in the content of the web page need to match or have some relevance to the search that was requested. Then the relevance of that content combined with the domain authority is used to determine where and on which page of the search results a website should appear.

There are specific hidden fields inside a web page that can be used to tell the search engine what a page is about—these are described as key words. If these special fields cannot be found then the search engine will look more closely at the title of the page and the content on the page to decide if the page is relevant to a search request or not.

Choosing the right key words to categorize each page in this way is absolutely critical to SEO. The goal is not just to find good descriptive key words that describe the page to a human; instead you want to match as closely as possible the keywords that people are really searching for using the search engines. There are many tools available to digital marketers that help them find the best keywords and rate the relevance of the keywords that are already being used.

Domain authority is like having a score for the importance of your website. Search engines have absolutely no idea if the content of a website is correct, or that the content of one website is more accurate than the content of any other website. Instead the search engines rely on counting the number of times third-party websites link to your website (and weighing the importance of those websites), the theory being that if lots of other important websites want to link to your website then your website must be an important influencer on a particular subject.

Therefore it is possible that your new website has great content, but is not appearing on the first page of Google's search results because the domain authority of this new website is very low.

Having an on-going programme for building good "back-links" to your website from authoritative third-party websites is good strategy to increase the domain authority of your website over time.

SEO gets more complicated when you consider the massive competition for good search result rankings. If your website enters a market with a high level of competition, and major established players that have already had 10 years to build up domain authority, then it will be difficult for your website to appear on the first page of Google with them. Thus, one of the roles of a digital marketer is to seek out other keywords that accurately describe your business, but for which competition is lower. Often this requires being very specific about your products or services. For instance, instead of being categorized as selling "books" you might change your keywords to "rare antique books from the 17th century".

Before 2010 it was believed that search engines could easily be swayed with false information to increase the chances of a website appearing on the first page of search results. However, in recent years search engines have evolved and are now able to identify shady SEO "tricks" and penalise websites employing black hat SEO (lowering such websites' rankings in search results). Accordingly, the only way to improve your search rankings today is to do so honestly. This often means having an ongoing website link building campaign.

There are two more key factors that play important roles in search results: the speed of your website and the ability to display the website properly on a smart phone. Failure to have a fast responding website that works equally well on a smart phone risks the search engine adding a penalty that will keep your website off page one.

As SEO is both a specialised skill and a time consuming ongoing activity, it is common for businesses to outsource this activity to a third party. According to a study by webpageFX.com in 2018, the monthly cost of SEO services from an agency can be anything from $500 to $5000 per month. The lower figure would be applicable to a 10 page business information website and the upper figure would be applicable to an e-commerce store with approximately 50,000 products. Freelance SEO rates for a similar quality service could be 25% cheaper.

Content marketing

Content marketing is an ongoing process where the online business aims to draw traffic to its website by publishing interesting articles that its potential customers want to read.

In addition to attracting new leads, content marketing is also powerful in engaging customers and growing a business brand.

This is usually achieved through posting articles on a blog that is under the same domain name as the business website. Staff then regularly write blog articles about subjects that interest the business's potential customers. A content marketing strategy will only work if the content is genuinely valuable to potential customers. It is not advisable to try to fake a content marketing strategy, as trust needs to be built with the readers.

An example of successful content marketing can be seen with hubspotcrm.com. The Hub Spot CRM is used by many small businesses, and so the content marketing for Hub Spot provides useful information on marketing for small businesses. The information shared is of very high quality, and is like an ongoing course on digital marketing shared between communities of people with similar goals.

Instead of writing blog articles, a content marketing strategy could also be implemented through publishing videos, white papers, photos, case studies and/or podcasts on a subject that will interest your potential customers. Almost any content format can be used as long as you shrewdly anticipate the information needs of your potential customers, and build a community around the brand.

Content marketers generally agree that it takes around 6 months of regular content marketing for a new business or new product before there are any visible results. Therefore content marketing can be treated only as a long term marketing strategy.

Email marketing

Email marketing aims to generate leads (or direct sales) through sending business emails to potential customers.

Despite the growth of social media. Emails remain the most used communication mechanism on the Internet. It is widely stated that in 2017, 90% of US adults used email compared to 70% of US adults that used social media.

Unlike social media marketing, you can "own" your email marketing audience. That is to say that on social media platforms you have no control over who receives your posts. For example, in recent years it has been increasingly obvious on Facebook that if you have a large number of friends and you post an update then Facebook makes a unilateral decision regarding which of your friends will receive that update. The update is not immediately received by all of your friends (followers). In comparison, when you have your own list of email addresses then you can send an email to each of those people, and they will all receive it. Furthermore, you don't need any platform to reach your audience beyond a simple email system. Consider also that if you have connections on a social media platform (e.g. LinkedIn), if your account is locked then you have no way of reaching those contacts outside of the social media platform.

There are two distinct email marketing approaches:

Direct email

Opt-in email

Direct email marketing is the email equivalent of telephone cold calling. The marketer has a list of potential leads. He then writes an email explaining the benefits of the product or service which is then sent by mail to each person on the list.

Opt-in email marketing differs in that the person being emailed has given their prior consent to be contacted. Opt-in email marketing requires first building an email list. The simplest approach is to add a newsletter sign-up form on your website. If you find that you don't get enough people to sign-up just for your newsletter then instead you may need to add an incentive by offering visitors something for free in exchange for signing up. This is called a "lead magnet". The freebie can be anything of value to the potential customers, for example a white paper, a check-list or a "how to" guide.

In contrast to direct marketing, the opt-in marketing approach is to only soft sell to your opt-in audience. This is achieved by sending helpful information, like a newsletter, which just happens to offer a discount when buying your product or service. If you send such an email then the call to action in the email should include a link to the product page on your website, so that the customer doesn't have to work too hard to make the purchase you are drawing them towards.

If you have anything other than a small email market audience then you will benefit from using a dedicated email marketing platform. The leading platforms are:

MailChimp

Constant Contact

AWeber

The benefit of using these tools is that when a visitor to your website signs up for your newsletter they are immediately added to your mail list on the email marketing platform. Then you can define email campaigns within the email marketing platform, and schedule them to run. The platform will provide detailed feedback on the status of your campaign, including how many mails were received and whether or not the call to action was clicked.

18. Increase visitors with social media marketing

Purpose

Social media marketing is the use of social media platforms (Facebook, Twitter, Instagram, LinkedIn etc.) to market products or services. This type of marketing can be more personal than traditional advertising (such as TV or radio advertising) because it creates a two way communication channel between the company and its audience. Anyone on the social media platform can choose to follow or be-friend the social media account of the company that they are interested in. When they receive broadcasts from the company account then they can reply and engage with the company.

Social media platforms have huge numbers of users. This makes them a good source of potential and existing customers.

The leading social media platforms by number of active users are:

Facebook: 2,130 million

YouTube: 1,500 million

Instagram: 800 million

Weibo: 376 million

Twitter: 330 million

Facebook is clearly the market leader with more than 2 Billion active users.

Source https://www.dreamgrow.com/top-15-most-popular-social-networking-sites/ April 2018.

Some social media websites, such as Facebook, offer specific business accounts that companies can create. Taking the example of Facebook, which allows a business to create its own business page within Facebook. This takes the form of a very simple business information website.

Using its Facebook business page the business can then post updates on the social media network for followers to receive. The updates are marketing messages crafted for use on that social media network. These updates can range from product and services promotions, to company updates (brand building), to messages intended to start a conversation with users or get their feedback on a subject.

The audience for a social media marketing campaign cannot be controlled, because anyone can choose to follow the company account. Therefore the likely audience will be potential customers, existing customers, journalists and bloggers. Engagement with journalists and bloggers is a good thing, because it can lead to distribution of the company's marketing messages to a wider audience.

Anyone on the social media platform who receives the marketing message can forward that message to other people within their social media network. Similarly, on most social media platforms it is possible to "like" a post that is viewed. When the post is "liked" then everyone within that person's social network gets notified. This is great news for an online business, because the company marketing message will be spread outside the business's existing network and be seen by more potential customers.

Social media marketing is not necessarily identical to content marketing. Pure content marketing involves publishing information valuable to potential customers on a topic that customers would find interesting. On social media the posts and updates could be such information, but could also be product promotions or simply company updates.

Social media offers public and private messaging. When a business posts an update then this update is received by all its followers or friends on the platform (ignoring some of the algorithmic restrictions imposed on accounts with huge numbers of followers). The followers can then add their own comments to the original post, or add comments to the last comment which would then be visible for all followers to see. Alternatively, a follower of the update can choose to send a private reply back to the account that sent the post.

Unlike more traditional forms of advertising, social media can be used to get customer feedback on new product ideas or even on existing products. This can be achieved by sending a quick survey to the social media followers or simply asking them to reply with their feedback.

As per the use of social media by individuals, the commercial use of social media is to build communities online. Good online communication in this way generates trust between consumers and the product or services supplier.

On social media each person's voice is not equal. There are online influencers who have worked hard to build audiences that trusts them and are interested to know what those influencers have to say. These influencers typically have large audiences. Therefore another social media marketing strategy is to market specifically to these online influencers. If the online influencer was to forward a promotional marketing post to his followers, then given his influence it might be read by many people and could result in good sales.

Advantages

The advantages of social media marketing include:

Low entry costs;

Access to large numbers of people;

Getting feedback from customers;

Timely;

Good engagement analytics.

All the leading social media platforms are free for businesses and individuals to create accounts.

As can be seen in the market share statistics above, the number of people who are active in social media is in the billions. All these people could receive your promotional material and could become your customers.

Social media is a two-way conversation. Recipients of posts can easily reply, giving their feedback on products, services or brands. Also, many platforms offer tools such as online survey creation to help you get answers from your audience.

Posting on social media can be very fast. There are no advertisement slots to be booked (for normal posts) or physical adverts to be made. This makes it very quick to reply in a timely fashion to industry or worldwide events.

Every social media platform has good built in analytics to track follower engagement. It is easy to see how many people received a post, liked the post or commented on it. This can be invaluable when deciding what type of content to post in the future for maximum engagement.

Disadvantages

The disadvantages of marketing with social media include:

Reputation damage;

Cost of engagement;

Difficult to measure Return on Investment (ROI).

What people see on social media can negatively affect your brand image. If you publish poor content then it can damage your brand image. Similarly, if someone replied to one of your posts stating that the claimed benefits of your product were false then that could destroy trust and reduce your sales.

Worse still, anyone online has the risk of being maliciously hacked. A hacker could gain access to your account and steal data, or steal your online identity and post malicious messages pretending to be you, all of which would damage your business reputation.

The true cost of engagement is not the free account opening, but much more the cost of the commitment to social media marketing. Without help from a dedicated marketing team, writing promotional material, publishing it on multiple social media platforms and following up on all replies can be very time consuming. Big companies will have dedicated teams for social media community engagement or will outsource this work.

It is difficult to measure the ROI of social media campaigns. The number of sales immediately following a campaign can be measured, but the value of long term brand building with customers could take years to result in sales.

19. Get visitors with online paid advertising

Why advertise online?

Having reached this chapter in the book you will already be aware of the large number of people using the Internet, and the number of different marketing techniques there are to reach those people for free. Given this information you may wonder why there is a chapter on online paid advertising.

The honest truth is that it takes time to reach your target audience. The best content marketing or social media marketing strategy is going to take months to build a strong following. If your business is reliant on making immediate sales to its online followers then this may take time you cannot afford. Furthermore, just building a following among people who are interested in what you have to say doesn't guarantee a high conversion rate from followers to sales.

Therefore an alternative or additional approach may be necessary to generate sales. This could be online paid advertising.

Online paid advertising includes the following:

Search engine advertising;

Social media paid advertising;

Online display advertising.

The following sections will explain these different types of advertising in more detail.

Search engine advertising

Search engine advertising aims to deliver paid adverts that are displayed on the same page as the search engine's organic search results. Typically the advert is a short sentence of text that when clicked redirects a user to your website. Therefore the advert is similar in appearance to the organic search results, although it will appear at the top of those search results and will be flagged as being an "Ad" or "sponsored".

Paid search engine advertising has been increasing year by year. In 2017 the global spend on search engine advertising was expected to exceed $90 Billion for the first time. Therefore not everyone is relying on organic search and content marketing to reach potential customers.

The leading search engine services (Google, Baidu and Bing) all offer the opportunity to pay to display an advert when a search engine user initiates a search containing specific keywords. This advertising service is open to anyone once they have created an advertising account with the search engine.

Deciding on the right keywords for the advert is crucial. The keywords can be identified in a very similar way to identifying keywords for SEO and organic searches. You would start by identifying words that define the product or service you want to advertise, then expand that set of keywords to all possible aliases and similar words.

The next step is to select your small set of advertising keywords from the long list that has just been created. To do this requires an understanding of the commercial aspects of search engine advertising.

As an advertiser you set a price that you are prepared to pay each time a search engine user clicks on your advert. When the user clicks they are redirected to the URL you defined when you submitted the advert; usually this a product or service purchase page on your website. If the advert is displayed (called an advert impression) but it is not clicked then you do not have to pay anything.

From the huge amount being spent globally on search engine advertising you can imagine that the competition to have adverts seen can be very high. The leading search engines make the most of this by inviting you to bid for advert placement based on your chosen keywords. As explained above, when you define your advert you can choose how much you wish to pay per click. If a similar advert placed by a different business proposes to pay more for each click then the search engine will have priority when the search engine decides which adverts to display.

Setting the right cost per click (CPC) is therefore very important. If the amount is too little then advertisers who are prepared to pay higher CPC will have their adverts shown instead. Alternatively, if you propose to pay a high CPC then you may be paying more than necessary for clicks, and eating into your profit margins. Luckily there are online tools to help decide what an appropriate CPC should be. You can enter your keywords and the tools will tell you how much people have paid recently for their adverts to be displayed with those keywords. Also, once you start your advertising campaign you will soon have your own advertising data and will be able to see whether or not your adverts are being displayed at the CPC you set.

Putting all this together, using your search engine advertising account you can create an online advertisement campaign. The campaign will consist of:

The advert short text;

URL to redirect to when clicked;

Pairs of keywords and CPC;

Daily or monthly budget.

The campaign can have more than one set of keywords, and each set will have defined its own CPC. Helpfully, advertising accounts allow you to set a budget by the day or by the month. This is a really useful safeguard against overspending, and I make use of this feature a lot for my own advertising.

Social media paid advertising

It is estimated that companies across the world will spend more than $30 billion on social media paid advertising in 2018. Therefore social media paid advertising is a major force in advertising, and is believed to already have overtaken global spending on newspaper advertising.

The leading social media platforms for business advertising are:

Facebook

Twitter

LinkedIn

Instagram

YouTube

Pintrest

Snapchat

The unique power of social media paid advertising is how precisely you can identify your target audience. With search engine advertising the target audience was defined as being those searching the web using particular words or phrases. In comparison, social media platforms allow an advert to be targeted more precisely using what the social media platform knows about the interests and career history of its members. This helps a social media advertiser reach groups of people without having to wait for those people to search for the advertiser's products. Compare the efficiency of this type of advertising to newspaper advertising or television advertising, where it is very difficult to target anything other than a very wide audience.

For example, on Facebook it is possible to target people who are living in a particular country, speak a particular language, are members of a particular Facebook group, are in a certain age range and are female. This is a simple example, and there are much more complex possibilities.

When advertising on social media there are typically a wide range of advert formats available—a much richer set of media formats than the short text sentence advert available with search engine advertising.

For example, Facebook supports the following advert formats:

Photo

Video

Carousel

Slide-show

Collection

Facebook also offers advert templates for a wide range of advertising purposes including:

Lead generation adds

Offers

Post engagement

Event responses

Page likes

The social media platform also allows the advertiser to choose where the advert will be placed on the page, e.g. in the user's news feed or on the right hand side bar. There are far more options in social media advertising than there are with search engine advertising.

Online display advertising

Display advertising is buying space on websites to display adverts. Most often the websites that have space for sale join an online advertising network, which will find buyers for their advertising space and will provide the technology to display the advert. Two of the leading online advertising networks are Google AdSense and Facebook Audience Network.

Adverts are submitted to the network by the advertiser, and it is the responsibility of the advertising network to find websites or mobile devices on which to display the adverts. The advertiser will define:

The target audience;

Advert creative (the design);

Schedule by which the advert is to be shown;

Price he is prepared to pay;

A total spending budget by day or by month.

Taking the example of Google AdSense, it is possible to define the target audience for your adverts in a number of ways. These include people showing interest in changing life events, people known to be already looking for certain product categories, completely custom audiences and re-targeting audiences.

The Google AdSense advert can be:

Text

Image

Video

Interactive media

On all advert display platforms, the size of the advert generally follows the Internet Advertising Bureau standard sizes which include:

Banners

Rectangles (of different sizes)

Leader boards

Pop-ups and pop-under

Two pricing categories are normally offered. The advertiser is either charged each time an advert is displayed (cost per impression) or each time an advert is clicked and redirects to the advertisers website (cost per click).

Most advertising display networks use a real time bidding process to decide which adverts get displayed at any point in time. The advertiser is not actively involved in the bidding. It is necessary only to define the price you are prepared to pay and the display advertising network automates the process from there.

Advert re-targeting

One other powerful feature of online advertising is termed re-targeting. This is a process whereby visitors to your website continue to receive adverts about your business through online advertising channels after they have left your website. Not every purchase follows the text book sequence of events, therefore reminding people of the purchase for which they visited your website, can lead the visitor towards a sale.

Both Google search engine marketing and Facebook social media marketing support advert re-targeting. They give you a piece of code that you embed in your website, which tracks visitors. Then when you define an advertising campaign with Google or Facebook you can choose the stored list of visitors as your target audience. This is quite easy because Facebook and Google already have the visitor information and therefore no additional data needs to be entered or uploaded.

20. Improve online success with analytics

Why use analytics?

You can improve your online success if you know what is happening online and are able to make changes that lead to improvements. This is a feedback loop where you deploy your services online, gather interaction metrics, make decisions from those metrics, make changes to your online services then redeploy them, start recording interactions again and repeat the cycle.

Using your own metrics you should be able to answer the following questions:

How many unique people visited the website?

How many people viewed each page or post?

Where are my visitors from?

How many people looked at the pricing page?

What was the ratio between numbers of visitors versus sales achieved.

Is the website being found on Google?

For an e-commerce website that is not making many sales, we could use the answers to these questions to decide if people are finding the website at all, and then at which point in the sales pipeline we are losing them. Accordingly we could decide where best to spend our time and money to get more sales. For example, if the number of unique visitors is low and the website is not visible in a Google search then we may decide to improve our SEO to get more visitors. Alternatively, if we are getting a large number of visitors to the website homepage and to the product pricing page, but very few sales then we need to look hard at the product pricing page and work out what on that page is putting people off from buying.

One of the many advantages of doing business online is being able to easily track who is engaging with your online services, and having readily available tools to help make business decisions based on such data.

This chapter will give you an explanation of how to track engagement across multiple platforms to help you make decisions about your online business.

Website interaction

Gone are the days when tracking interaction on your website was limited to a page visit counter. If you only count page visits then you have no way of knowing how many unique people visited the website, where those people came from, how long they spent on each page and the sequence of pages that they went through.

I would recommend that everyone considers using Google Analytics to track interactions on their websites. This is the most used website analytics tool on the internet, and you can use it forever on the free tier if you wish.

To add Google Analytics to your website all that you will need is a Google Analytics account, and then to add a tiny code snippet to each web page (easily achieved on platforms like WordPress by using a ready-made plugin). Then every time someone visits one of your pages their visit is recorded by Google (nothing is stored on your own website or hosting account).

In order to view the analytics you simply login to your account at "http://analytics.google.com". Once logged in you can see summary information, define and view dashboards or drill down into more detailed data.

Analytics immediately available will include:

The number of unique visitor sessions by day;

Number of page views per page;

How long a visitor stayed on each page;

The country, language and browser of the visitor.

The Google Analytics online tools can be used to obtain in-depth analytics of your choosing, such as how many people from each country visited a specific page, and what was the average time they spent on the page.

This information can also be very useful if you are doing content marketing from your own website (not from social media), because you can use the analytics to learn which of your posts is getting the most interest. Bloggers often find that some of their posts receive an order of magnitude more readers than the rest of their posts. It is important to find which of your posts are popular in this way so that you can learn from it and aim to repeat the success.

The technology used by Google Analytics does not noticeably reduce the performance of your website.

Website replay

The information available from Google Analytics is often enough to pinpoint the page in your sales sequence on which visitors leave your website and don't buy your product, but there will not be enough information to show you exactly what happens when they are on that page.

If your online business is at the stage where you are getting visitors, but you are not getting the outcome that you want, then it is worth looking at tools that allow website replay.

The leading tools that provide website replay service are:

Mouseflow

HotJar

FullStory

Each one of these tools works differently, but the end result is similar and they are direct competitors. Installation is similar to that for Google Analytics, with insertion of a simple tracking code. Each of the aforementioned website replay tools offer a limited free plan, with more features available if you pay a monthly subscription.

The benefits of using these tools over statistical analytics include:

Replaying the session of a visitor;

Creating heat maps of page use;

Seeing where each individual visitor came from.

The whole session of a visitor, across the multiple pages they visited, can be replayed for you to watch as if it was a video of the visitor's screen. This replay can give you amazing insights into how your pages are being used and whether visitors even reach a certain part of your page. You can watch the movement of the visitor's mouse across the screen and see the letters typed into your online forms. Replay works for both mobile and desktop visits.

Heat maps are a visual summary of all the web sessions that have been recorded. You can look at a particular page and from the heat map colours know instantly where your visitors are spending their time on each of your pages. Conversely, you can also see which parts of your pages are rarely visited, and this could give you the information you need to understand why you are not getting the sales you expected.

Each recording also has some information about the user. For example you can see the country and the city of the user, as well as the web page from which they came from.

Social media interaction

Each social media platform has its own built-in statistical analytics that are available for you to see. Typical available information would be how many people have seen a particular post or page, how many people liked the page (clicked on the "like" button), and how many people shared your post with their network.

This information can be very useful to help understand which subjects are getting the most attention from your readers. As a result you might then decide to change how some of your posts are written to increase the engagement with new posts in the future.

Unfortunately, unlike the website analytics tools discussed in previous sections, social media analytics will not give you detailed information on who visited your page or post. This is one of the drawbacks of social media platforms—they are closed systems that ultimately "own" their audiences. Only by using your own website will you get more detailed information about your online audience.

Search engine information

Search engines can also give you useful information if you have registered yourself as the website owner. Some of this information is quite technical. However, seeing any errors can you give you a clue as to why your pages are not appearing in online searches or why they have such low rankings.

Taking the example of Google Search Console (which can be found within the suite of tools known as the Google Webmaster Tools). With the console you can look separately at each of the websites you have registered. The information available for each website includes:

Errors found when analysing the website pages;

Which key words people used to find your website;

Which websites link to your website;

Any mobile usability errors;

Security issues;

Any penalties applied to the website ranking.

Even if you are not a search engine expert, looking at these tools should give you some hints as to whether or not things are working properly. Any errors are worth investigating as the search engines are a good low cost source of visitors for your website.

21. How to engage digital professionals

Who do you need to hire?

At this stage you may have decided that you need some external help to get your online strategy implemented. Often for small businesses it is not cost-effective to hire permanent staff to build a website. Therefore, this chapter will cover engaging people for temporary assignments.

You could consider engaging any one of the following:

A well-known digital agency;

A small digital agency;

One web professional;

A team of freelancers;

A mixture of freelancers and your team.

A digital agency is a business that undertakes any digital work for its clients. A digital agency employs its own digitally-skilled staff to cover: web design, web development, digital marketing and online advertising. Engagement with a digital agency to build something typically involves a fixed price contract with one person appointed to manage your project. For ongoing SEO or website maintenance from a digital agency a further fixed price monthly package would be purchased.

Freelancers in the context of this book are self-employed people who have specific skill sets either for web design, web development, project management or digital marketing.

A web professional is a freelancer who has skills in web design, web development, project management and digital marketing.

The first decision you will need to make is whether to ask a digital agency to help implement your online strategy or whether to hire freelancers instead. In my opinion the main factors in this decision should be:

Your budget;

How comfortable you are with managing people;

Personal referrals.

You would expect the web designs from a well-known agency to be first class and very original. A well-known digital agency will do everything by the book and you are likely to receive sketch designs, web page mock-ups and other documents throughout the life cycle of the project. These are all value-adding best practices, but they cost. The agency has a reputation to keep, and will not be interested in producing a simple boilerplate solution.

A big well-known digital agency also needs a big budget. The clients of well-known digital agencies are typically large corporations that want a complete solution with minimal involvement. These corporations are prepared to pay well based on the expectation that they will get a high quality solution. Despite the cost, if you have already seen the work of a particular agency, and you have had personal referrals from people you trust then it could be a good choice to work with that agency.

Alternatively, if you want the benefits of working with one organisation that can deliver a complete solution, but on a smaller budget, then you may find a small digital agency that you would like to work with. One of the advantages of a digital agency is that you only have to deal with one organisation, whereas the alternative for a big website project might be to have to hire multiple freelancers and then manage those freelancers yourself. A small agency is more likely to tailor its process to suit your budget, so it will not produce all the documentation that you would expect from a well-known agency, and instead you will be expected to review the work yourself and share your opinions. It is likely to be a more interactive experience.

Before we consider how to hire a team of freelancers, let's consider as an alternative the engagement of a web professional. If your web project is manageable by one person, or more accurately you know of someone who has all the necessary skills and you believe the delivery of their solution will be possible within your desired time frame, then a web professional could be a good choice. A web professional is likely to have experience working with many different clients, and can tailor their working approach to suit your situation. Depending on your budget the process can be as light as you want, or as close to best practices as you need.

If you are willing to get involved in the hiring, then a team of freelancers can be a very cost-effective solution. The advantage is that you engage an expert for each area: a web developer, a digital marketing expert, a web designer and perhaps a project manager. A project manager can save you a lot of effort (for an additional cost); if you intend to hire a project manager then it may be a good idea to engage him first, and then ask him to recruit the rest of the team (or at least help you recruit the rest of the team). The downside of this approach is that you are creating a new team that has never worked together before. There is a risk that there will be friction within the team if not everyone gets along together, or that the team will take time learning how best to work together. You may be able to leave this problem to the project manager, otherwise you may need to get involved more.

Paying a team of freelancers can be by the hour or fixed price. If it is fixed price then either you or the project manager would need to define the work clearly enough for each freelancer that the freelancer could then propose a fixed price or be able to tell you if they accept the fixed price you have proposed. In this situation you may need to be flexible on payment if the freelancers believe that they have completed their jobs, but your website is not finished and there were mitigating circumstances. Conversely, if you can't define the work completely enough for a fixed price contract then an hourly contract will be the best approach, but this shouldn't stop you from asking for planned hours of work and from managing your own budget.

The final alternative is a hybrid approach where you hire one specific freelancer, and you or your team do the rest of the work. This can be a good solution if you have a very clear vision of what you want to achieve, you are happy to get involved and the scope of what you want to achieve is limited. For example, you may want to build a business information website in WordPress with a specific design template (a WordPress theme), and all you need is a freelance web developer with WordPress expertise to build the business website for you. The design will not be original because a publicly-available design template is being used; the advantage is that you will not need a web designer. However, someone will need to do the digital marketing, so you can either do that yourself or hire another freelancer as necessary. This is likely to be a very cost effective approach.

Where can these people be found?

Any well-known digital agency will have its own website. Therefore you could search for them online and send them a brief summary of what it is you want them to do, then wait for them to contact you.

Less well known digital agencies could also be found by searching for digital agencies online. On their websites they are likely to have a client list or a list of previous projects. Reading about their clients, past projects and the profile of the agencies should tell you quite quickly if the agencies regularly work with businesses of your size or not.

Be prepared for the questions that you may be asked by digital agencies before any work starts. Sometimes a digital agency will have a detailed online form that you need to fill in to explain your project before the agency will contact you. Questions on the form will help the digital agency know more about your project before speaking with you, and will also help the agency screen out customers that it doesn't want to do business with. For example, you might be asked straight away what your budget is ,and if you have big ideas but little money then the agency may choose not to take your enquiry any further.

Small digital agencies can also be found on internet freelance websites. Such websites are also the main source of freelancers of any kind. These are specific digital economy market places that specialise in matching staff with customers looking to deliver online projects (e.g. websites).

Unless you already know freelancers that you want to work with, the best approach to hiring freelancers is to use a freelance website.

Hiring on freelance websites

Some countries have specific niche freelance websites (often in the local language), however there are also huge freelance websites that are international and where all business is conducted in English. The leading global freelance websites include:

Upwork

Guru

Freelancer

We Work Remotely

Fiverr

People Per Hour

Fiverr is a special case on this list. As its name suggests, this freelancer portal matches customers with freelancers for small packaged jobs that start at five dollars. This is a little like shopping from a restaurant menu, rather than having to explain your tastes in food and finding a restaurant that will help you. For example, you might find someone who will install a WordPress theme for you on your existing WordPress website for a fixed cost.

The downside of using Fiverr is the risk of paying very little for something which you know is an order of magnitude more expensive elsewhere, and then expecting the result to be of equal quality. For example, you might find someone offering to build a complete website for £50. It sounds amazing but don't be surprised if the final delivery is nothing like what you expected.

Other than that, the remaining freelance websites on the list work differently. All of them have two methods of working in common:

Finding a freelancer;

Sourcing staff for a project.

If you are simply looking for the right freelancer then you can use these freelance websites to find a freelancer who is currently available and has the skills that you need. Therefore, before you start searching you need to know which types of freelancers you need (e.g. web developer or web designer) and the specific technologies with which they may need to have expertise (e.g. experienced with Weebly or skilled in marketing on Facebook). You will then get a long list of people, with their hourly rates, a list of all their skills, testimonies from previous engagements and a mini CV. Through the freelance website you can then send a freelancer a message and start to evaluate if they would be a good fit for the project you are planning.

The second method for engaging freelancers on the portal is to write a description of the project you wish delivered, and then to publish the project description for everyone on the freelance website to see. Soon after, you should receive replies through the website from freelancers who will either ask for more information or will quote the price they are willing to accept to deliver the project. When you submit your project description you can choose to include your budget. This can be useful as it can help you screen out candidates who are too expensive or have completely misunderstood the scale of the project.

My advice on how to accept freelance proposals is to not enter into a race to the bottom. The freelancers on the website will come from all over the world. As a result some people will be genuinely cheaper than others and you can find a bargain, however there will also be people to whom $20/day is a lot of money but who don't have the skills to deliver what you want.

Time is not infinite and litigation will not get your project delivered. With both of the freelancer selection methods we've discussed, it is best to identify freelancers that you can comfortably communicate with, who have a track record of delivering projects, claim to have the skills you need and are proposing to work for a price that you believe is fair. To ensure that you can communicate with them, read their proposal, chat with them online and reach a conclusion. Your chosen freelancer website will list the skills that the freelancers have. Cross reference this list with the skills that you need, and the skills the freelancers would have needed to have for the projects they claimed to have completed in their online histories.

Unfortunately, the freelance website will restrict your communication with the freelancer, because the website wants to protect its fees, which are at risk if you decide to work with the freelancer outside of the freelance website platform. Therefore many of these websites will not let you know the full name or email address of the freelancer. This is a pain because it stops you from searching for the freelancer elsewhere online and seeing if there are any positive or negative reviews about them.

If you doubt a freelancer's skills then either don't engage them through the website, or ask someone else to evaluate them for you. In most cases there will be so many freelancers that match your skill criteria that you can simply skip anyone about whom you have doubts.

To confuse matters, if you publish a project description then you will get replies from individual freelancers as well as from companies (small digital agencies). You will need to think differently when evaluating companies. For instance, a company representative who sends you a freelancer proposal is not likely to be the person at the company who actually does the work. Instead the person who contacts you is probably the commercial manager or project manager. This is okay, but be aware that it is not this contact person's technical skills that you want to evaluate. Furthermore, if you request a technical discussion then you could end up speaking with anyone at the company who is skilled and available, but there will be no commitment that this same person will be the one working on your project. Therefore, in this situation I would rely more on the company's understanding of your project (do they ask the right questions?), the past projects the company has performed on the freelance website and the ratings that previous clients have given the company.

Give a thought also to the location in which the freelancers are based, and the amount of interaction you will need to have with them. For instance, if you know that your project will require regular live meetings, with screen sharing and discussions then you need to engage freelancers that have working hours that overlap with yours; otherwise your communication may only happen through messaging. In contrast, if all that you need is some website forms created and you can specify exactly how the forms will work then you may never need to speak to the person, and messaging will suffice.

When you have decided whom you want to engage then you need to execute the engagement through the freelance website. In most cases the proposal made to you will be structured to include a deposit and a final payment. To start the engagement you will need to pay the deposit, which is held in escrow until the work is finished. At the end of the project you pay the balance and take the finished project. In a dispute you would ultimately lose the deposit, but not make the final payment. Disputes are settled by the freelance website staff and you will not have the opportunity to involve an external third party.

Don't forget that the people you have engaged are completely unknown to you. Because the freelance website doesn't let you have their full names or their contact details you have very few options if they do anything malicious. For example, you may give them access to install a new website on your hosting server. When the project is complete, unless you block their server account or change the passwords, then there is a risk that they can later access your server and do some damage. Luckily this is very rare, but it is better to think about protecting your security before giving any freelancer access.

Here follows a summary of the key steps discussed in the this chapter to engage staff for your project.

Engaging staff for your project

1. Decide on the roles
2. Local or remote?
3. Agency or freelancers?
4. Propose/discuss requirements
5. Verify skills
6. Contract

22. How to work with your web team

Remote working

When you hire freelancers then in most cases they will work remotely across the Internet, and not in your office. They maybe in the same country as you or on the other side of the world, but either way it is unlikely that they will have included any travel costs in their proposals. Most freelancers will never meet their clients face to face (or feel the need to do so).

If this way of working is new to you then let me explain how it works. The key to working remotely is to use tools that can replace the different types of communication that would happen if you were in the same office as together.

First of all make sure there is a plan that everyone agrees to. This may be as simple as planning that the one person you engaged will start on Monday and finish in two weeks. However, I would advise also having an agreed-upon delivery plan, so that there is a shared view on when deliveries will be made, as this makes it easier for you to know how the project is progressing.

Business analysis conducted remotely has three stages. The first stage is collecting your business information, which can be achieved by sending documents by email, discussing how things work on the telephone and answering questions by email. The second stage is the creation of a business analysis document (written remotely). Finally, the document will be shared with you by email and then reviewed by email or by phone.

Designing the solution can be harder, because it is natural that there is a degree of interactivity. If the project brief does not contain enough information then the web designer is going to need to ask questions by email or by phone until he has enough detail to create a rough sketch of the web pages that will become the front end of the website. These sketches need to be shared by email, which means that they could be drawn by hand then scanned, or created in a slide show tool or Photoshop. If the design then needs to be discussed interactively the easiest approach is to use a conferencing tool (e.g. Skype), and for the designer to share his screen so that you can see it and comment on it while he notes the changes during the conversation.

Back-end designs (e.g. databases or booking engines) won't need to be shared for your review, although it would be useful to make sure that all parties are in agreement regarding the requirements and the design objectives.

While the website is being built, I would suggest that the web developer shows you what the real pages look like as soon as he has something to show. Even if you only receive a website link by email with no commentary, at least that would help you to see if the website is progressing as expected. This feedback should be repeated regularly until the website is complete. During this time do ask for updates on the expected delivery date, as it may have changed.

You and your team must have access to the finished website in order to approve it. To do this you will need an explanation of how to use it (especially the back-end if it is complicated), which could be communicated in an email, a slide show or a show and tell screen sharing session. It is unlikely that you will find everything working perfectly the first time, so it is best to prepare for this. To get maximum efficiency out of your project team I would suggest taking a screen capture of every issue you see and annotating it (if not clear) before sending the issue to the web developer by email. Keep a list of all the errors you find, and use this as a check-list when reviewing later releases.

Once you have approved the website then the web team should deploy it to your hosting environment and prepare it for the go-live. The web team can do this remotely. No special tools are needed for this on your side.

Often issues are detected in the days immediately following the go-live. Ideally your web team will have a tool in place to track the issues that you or your customers report; if not, then a spreadsheet could be used for this.

In summary using these simple tools can contribute to the success of your project:

Messaging or email;

Video conferencing with screen sharing;

Drawing tools (e.g. Photoshop);

Screen capture tool for screen shots;

Issue tracking system;

Spreadsheets.

If you used a freelance website platform to engage your project team then the platform may impose its own restrictions on the tools you use. For example, if the platform doesn't allow email addresses to be shared then you will have to use the messaging tool that is part of the platform.

When you are used to having your staff sitting in the same office as you then one of the most difficult issues when your team is working remotely is knowing exactly how many hours the team has worked. Clearly this problem is not insurmountable, because millions of people work remotely every day, but it can lead to doubts and mistrust. My advice would be to first consider whether you really need to use hours of work as a measurement; for instance you could work on fixed price contracts if it makes you more comfortable. Another approach is to ask for estimates before agreeing to the work. Then you can question the final hourly bill from the freelancer if there is a major discrepancy; the freelancer will know this and having given an estimate he will be smart enough to keep you up to date on any time overrun. Also, if you hired a project manager then you can rely on his time tracking for the whole team.

Signs of trouble to come

Whether your web project team is right next to you, or on the other side of the world, here are some warning signs to look out for that may indicate that the delivery of your project is at risk.

No communication received;

You never understand each other in conversation;

You never get what you ask for;

It takes days to get answers to your questions;

The person you engaged doesn't remember the last conversation you had;

Deliveries are getting late.

If the project has started but you don't receive any communication from the web project team for a number of days then I would be concerned. Ideally you would have already agreed that you would be in touch or deliver something within a number of days, so if they exceed those agreed dates and there is still no communication then it is certainly time to chase them.

The second issue happens mostly with freelancers whose first language is not the same as your own. They agree to everything, but when you ask more probing questions they are unable to answer. Sometimes with the same freelancer interactive conversation is difficult, but email conversation has been fine. This was probably because they had more time to answer the email. In this situation it is good to find a communication method that works best for both of you rather than losing time changing the freelancer. However, if the freelancer cannot understand you at all then they will not be building what you asked for, because they could never have really understood what you wanted. In this situation, seriously consider swapping out the freelancer or bringing in a project manager who speaks the same language as the freelancer.

If you never get what you ask for in early deliveries, and if nothing improves then you can be sure that you will not be pleased with the final delivery either. This could be a simple communication problem or it could be a lack of skills. If it is a skill problem then replace the freelancer as soon as possible.

It can take days to get answers to questions. This may not necessarily become a risk to the final delivery. Look to see if there are any other issues in the project. Is the web team focussed only on delivery, and is poor on customer service? If they don't understand your questions then treat it as a communication failure (see above).

Sometimes when working with freelancers you have a good conversation (usually by email or messaging in this case), and then the next day the same person doesn't seem to remember anything you discussed previously. With remote workers this is a sign that you are not working with a single freelancer, but with a company that has a pool of people that they assign to your work as the company sees fit. Clearly changing a developer or a designer every day is not going to be efficient. Furthermore this is an indication that the people you engaged are not entirely honest, which is not a good sign for the long term. My experience with this has always been where English language has been a problem, in which case I have been quite direct and told the person they need to come back today with a delivery date for the feature we were just discussing. This has worked so far because it gives them time to talk to the right people in their own language, and then to come back with a realistic answer, but in this situation I wouldn't be keen to give the company repeat business.

If deliveries are getting late then you already have a problem. It is a good time to ask for the plan (or the final delivery date on less structured projects) to be re-estimated so that you can see the real impact of the delays. In a software project it is very unlikely that you can make the time up somewhere else unless you cancel some of the target functionality. Assuming the project is quite advanced at this stage then apart from displaying your displeasure there is often not much you can do but to accept the delays, and not forget the delays when it comes to giving feedback on the freelancer website or considering them for future projects.

23. We went live—what happens next?

Your website is live and visitors are coming to it—what happens next?

View your analytics

Your website is only serving its purpose if people are visiting it. Look at the analytics you have set-up (e.g. on Google Analytics) to see where visitors are coming from, which pages they have viewed and how close they are getting to placing orders (on an e-commerce website).

Within a few days of the website being launched you should start to see some visitors, even if these are search engine robots. If not, then something maybe wrong. On a website with a sequence you expect people to follow (e.g. a sales sequence on an e-commerce website) then look at the visitor numbers for each part of the sequence and see if you can make improvements to get the visitors to follow to the end of the sequence.

Look for errors

Someone needs to look for errors.

Either you or your web developer need to look at your search engine account (e.g. Google Webmasters) and see if your website has been indexed yet. Identify if there are any search errors that need to be fixed. Once the search engine has found your website then you can also look at the back-links and internal links, and check that they are what you expect them to be (e.g. no spam and no missing links).

You won't get to the top of Google's search rankings for categories if there are errors indexing your website or if Google is applying penalties because it doesn't like what it finds.

Your web developer needs to be regularly looking at your website log files and fixing any errors that are found. You may have both hosting error files and web application error files (e.g. WordPress is likely to be configured to have its own log files). You may be losing visitors when they click on your web page links and see errors ; you will be able to see this from the log files. If your website is a replacement for an old website you had on the same domain name then previous visitors may have bookmarked pages from the old website and are now unable to find them. This issue can be identified from the log files, and a suitable redirection put in place so that the visitors get to see your new home page instead of receiving an error.

Are emails coming through? Verify that when your website thinks it is sending emails that they really do get sent. This may be a technical configuration problem that is outside of your control, as on many shared hosting platforms the hosting provider imposes spam filters that can block the email you are trying to send. Use your "contact us" page and try to send yourself a message from the website.

Is the website up and working? Someone in your team needs to be alerted if your website is not available for visitors. Problems, like technical failures or Denial of Service attacks, could happen at any time. There are a number of automated solutions for this. For example Status Cake (https://www.statuscake.com/) has a free tier for monitoring a small number of websites and sending an email alert when the website doesn't respond.

Is everything still working on different browsers? In the world of website software, just because something worked once in testing doesn't mean it is going to work in exactly the same way on the public Internet. Reassure yourself by trying the website with different browsers and from mobile devices.

Can users see all your products? If you are using a CMS or some other web application to implement your e-commerce store then double check that all the products you wanted to put on sale are really visible online. This applies also to product variants, for example if you sell t-shirts then check that all the colours and sizes that you want to offer are really visible.

Data maintenance

Make sure that the responsibilities and processes are clear for keeping your website up to date. For instance, if you have a website selling services then who is going to add new services to your website or remove them if they are no longer available? If your e-commerce store only promotes your products when it thinks they are in stock, then be sure that someone is keeping the inventory up to date. Ideally this is something that you or your team are going to do, and not something that requires you to book time with your web developer. As you will remember, having control over the content yourself is one of the reasons why so many people use a CMS or an e-commerce platform instead of a plain HTML website.

Check if you have these five ticking time bombs

No backups;

Low on disk space;

Website slows right down at the same time each day;

Inability to handle increases in transaction volumes;

Poorly written code leading to long term maintenance.

Now that your website is live and your business reputation is at stake, make sure that regular website and database backups are taking place. These backups are your final defence against external attacks or your hosting company being unable to provide you with a service.

As you website gets successful, with more visitors and more products, you may start to run low on disk space. When you run out then your website will stop working. Someone in your team needs to watch this.

Regular slow performance of a website at a particular time of day can be a sign of bigger problems to come. There are all sorts reasons for this, ranging from your own hosting not being powerful enough any more to other websites on the same shared web hosting platform slowing down your website.

You may find that at any time of day your website can't manage more than a certain number of customers buying at the same time. This could be a complex problem to resolve. Sometimes it is due to the way in which the website software was built, and however much extra hosting power you give it the problem won't go away. In these situations you need to look to migrate to a better solution. For example, this could be the point at which you find that the e-commerce plugin you are using on WordPress just can't deliver what your business needs any more, and it is time to replace the whole website with a custom solution.

Poorly written software inside your website can lead to costly maintenance later on. Your website might look beautiful, but if your developers cut corners and didn't follow industry best practices then it may become expensive to make simple changes. If you reach this stage and it is key to your business to deliver changes to your website very quickly then it might already be time to consider a website replacement.

24. Case studies

Business information website

For the first case study, let me recount the creation of my own business information website.

The website was conceived when it became apparent that potential clients were looking for examples of my work online. So even though the website was built to attract new clients that had never heard of me, in fact the first audience the website was built to assist was people who already had some knowledge of what I do.

One of the most difficult activities in this web project was deciding which business lines to show on the website and which to leave out. This issue arose from the conflicting views of wanting to show specialisation in certain areas (not being a jack of all trades), while also communicating the many different lines of business that I was involved in. For example, I write books and I also consult on web projects. In the end, I opted for showing a limited number of business lines to communicate clearly that I do different things, while still showing that there is depth to each line. Thinking about the "knowledge architecture" of the website took a few days before I was happy with it.

The name of the website was relatively easy to decide upon, because the website is about me so it had to involve my name. That said, more recently I have seen examples individuals successfully promote themselves with websites that don't use their first and last names in the websites names.

Then the first website was built in an afternoon and went live on an economy shared hosting environment.

Within 6 months I needed to update the website and found that it was a pain to regularly edit html files. I was making mistakes, which were leading to poor website user experience. At that time I had built a number of WordPress websites for clients, and so it seemed a natural progression to replace my handmade HTML website with a WordPress one. This also allowed me to add dynamic information that changes regularly (e.g., the consultancy projects I am working on), which I would not have done on my old website.

The WordPress replacement took no more than an afternoon of intense labour. It uses a free WordPress theme and free WordPress plugins, and has therefore been very cost efficient.

Within the first year the website was noticeably slow at certain times in the day (not always the same times). Therefore I made the decision to migrate the website from a very basic economy shared hosting plan to a VPS. I was really pleased with the performance improvement, and have noticed that the speed is now fairly consistent across the day.

The website has served its purpose, although when I look at it again now I am painfully aware that the design needs to be updated!

Event Ticketing

A client asked me to build him a website for selling e-tickets to the events that he was already hosting (car shows, fireworks, Christmas activities). Having done my research, I identified a commercial paid WordPress plugin that would provide the ticketing functionality. After discussion with the client on the pros and cons of building our own solution we settled on the commercial plugin.

I ran tests on the ticketing plugin to be sure that it supported the functionality that had been requested. At that stage everything looked good.

The modified website went live just before the new season started. Within a week of selling tickets the first major problems occurred. Customers were reporting that their tickets were not arriving by email as they should have. In the beginning this looked like human error, where people may have incorrectly entered their email addresses. However, as the number of issues of this kind rose it was clear that the problem was the technical solution being used.

After a few stressful weeks of this, and many irate customers, we managed to get to the bottom of the problem. The shared hosting provider had very strict rules for identifying spam emails. After many technical discussions we found out that the hosting provider was automatically dropping many of the emails being sent. But we were not getting any warnings about this.

The hosting provider was unwilling to change its spam detection rules, because that would have affected tens of thousands of other shared hosting accounts. So we soldiered on with a number of workarounds to resend emails manually through our personal email accounts when necessary.

This situation then got worse when the volume of ticket sales increased. The website itself was then pausing for minutes before displaying pages. The worst of this was happening when the event customers were trying to checkout their ticket purchases. With only a month left in the fairly short season for these event tickets it was time to take action.

Having discussed it with the hosting provider, we first upgraded to a managed WordPress environment. This put the website on a much more powerful server. Some things did work better, but the crucial checkout activity was not much better and the customer complaints continued.

Next we upgraded to an even more powerful VPS, but the checkout performance problem continued. This seemed like complete madness. We had upgraded from a tiny £5/month hosting platform to an enormous £36/month monster, and still the problems persisted.

When we were using shared hosting the technical support was excellent, but confusingly once we migrated to a VPS with the same hosting provider we didn't get any technical help at all. They said that the VPS was a professional level solution, and it was up to us to do our own technical support. Despite all these problems we limped through to the end of the season.

The work to build the event website with the plugin was achieved by one web professional in less than 2 months. There were no specific SEO requirements, as the business already had a successful internet following.

The next year the ticketing plugin was replaced by a monthly subscription to the Coconut Tickets online ticketing platform. No more slow response issues were reported and (apart from human error) everyone got their e-tickets by email. Furthermore, the client's overall monthly cost was less than with the original event website running on the VPS.

In summary, the final outcome was a success but it was a long and stressful road getting there.

3D printing store

This was a project to build a complete 3D printing internet store for purchasing 3D printing materials and also for ordering 3D prints online.

The business owner had a good idea of what he wanted and had seen competitors' websites that were very impressive. Unfortunately, he didn't have the budget to match what I believe his competitors had spent when building their bespoke solutions.

Instead the best approach was to build a WordPress solution, using a free e-commerce store theme and then developing any missing features. This included the complete development of the module for taking 3D printing orders, as that feature was not available commercially at the time.

The website itself has since been redesigned around 10 times to make it as attractive as possible, while being as easy to use for the printing customers as possible. The current version of the website looks really great, although it has taken 2 years of incremental improvement to get this far. I expect that the makers of the WordPress theme would not recognise their design any more, as almost everything has been replaced or customized.

It also took more than 12 months before the number of weekly sales reached double digits. One of the main drivers to increasing the number of sales has been a regular content marketing campaign on social media, where the business owner has grown his authority while also growing his brand and increasing traffic to his website. As a result, a blog has been added to the printing website to further increase content marketing.

The work was conducted by one freelance web developer and one freelance SEO expert. In addition, the business owner has played a big role in designing the appearance of the website, defining the knowledge architecture and doing all the content management.

In summary, the website has been a success although it has taken time to get this far. Despite the time taken I strongly believe that the complete project has cost much less than the solutions built by his competitors.

~~

Thank-you for reading my book. If you enjoyed it and you found it useful, then please take a moment to leave me a review for this book on your retailer's website.

Thanks!

Clive Verrall

cliveverrall.com

25. Glossary

Affiliate marketing: promoting the products of a third party in return for sales commission.

B2B: business to business.

B2C: business to customer (a retail business).

Big data: looking for patterns in extremely large data sets, especially to understand human behaviour.

Blog: a website for publishing articles to read.

Botnet: a network of software robot website attackers.

C2C: customer to customer (customers sell to other customers).

CMS: Content Management System; a tool for building websites with dynamic information.

Content marketing: promotion through the distribution of useful online information.

CPC: cost per click.

CRM: Customer Relationship Management system.

DDoS: Distributed Denial of Service Attack.

Dedicated server: a real physical server that is not shared with anyone else.

Deployment: the process of installing new software before a go-live.

Digital agency: sells services to help others achieve their digital strategy.

Digital store: like an online store but only for digital products.

Digital strategy: how your business plans to operate in the digital economy.

Display advertising: buying space on websites to display adverts.

Domain authority: a measure of the importance of your website.

Domain name: the words used to address your website e.g., "example.com".

DoS: Denial of Service attack.

Drop shipping: delivering products bought online just in time without holding inventory.

Drupal: an open-source CMS framework for building sophisticated websites.

E-commerce: doing business online, typically the buying and selling of products.

Email marketing: generating leads through sending business emails to potential customers.

Freelancer portal: a place to find freelancers online.

Freelancer: someone who works for themselves.

GDPR: European General Data Protection Regulation.

Go-live: switching on the delivered service at the end of a project.

Google AdSense: a leading online advertising network run by Google.

HTML: Hyper Text Markup Language, the low level code of websites.

Impression: the event of displaying an advert online.

IT: Information Technology, providing business solutions using computers.

Joomla: an alternative open-source CMS to WordPress.

Keyword: a word used by a website to describe the contents of its page when being searched by a search engine.

Lead magnet: a gift offered in return for declaring an interest in a subject.

LMS: Learning Management System, a platform that runs courses for people to learn from.

Magento: an open-source e-commerce website building platform.

Managed VPS: a VPS sold with technical support.

Membership websites: websites that you need to be a member of to use.

Online auctions: an auction to bid for products/services completely online.

Online booking: buying tickets on the Internet.

Online learning: facilities for learning on the Internet.

Online store: an internet website from which physical products can be bought.

Online strategy: the websites, mobile applications and email communications that are part of your digital strategy.

Open source software: publicly accessible software that can be freely shared.

Payment gateway: the connection between your system and the payment system.

PayPal: a leading online payment services provider.

PCI DSS: Payment Card Industry Data Security Standard.

Photoshop: Adobe Photoshop is a graphics and photo editor.

SaaS: Software as a Service.

SEO: Search Engine Optimization, the process of improving a website such that it can be found easily by search engines.

Shared hosting: servers shared between different website owners.

Shopify: an e-commerce website building and hosting tool.

SQL injection: a type of website hacking attack.

SSL: secure sockets layer, protects the communication between your website and any visitor.

Stripe: a leading online card payment services provider.

UAT: user acceptance testing, the process by which a business owner tests and accepts (or rejects) a major delivery.

URL: the address of a world wide web page.

VPS: Virtual Private Server, your own server hosting space on a hosting platform.

Web designer: someone who designs how a website looks (a graphical designer).

Web developer: the person who builds websites.

Web professional: someone who aims to combine the roles of web developer, web designer, web project manager and SEO.

Web-server: the software infrastructure that displays websites to visitors.

Website builder: an online tool used to create a website.

Website project manager: someone who manages a complete web project, the project team and external dependencies.

Weebly: an open source website building tool for non-technical users.

WIX: a commercial website building tool for non-technical users.

WordPress plugins: third-party functionality extensions to WordPress.

WordPress themes: third-party website design templates.

WordPress: the most used website building system in the world today.

~~

26. About the Author

Clive Verrall has a long history of web projects, starting from putting his first commercial website on the Internet in 1997 while working for a European banking group, to being the founder of the e-ticketing specialist Coconut Tickets in 2016.

The author has been working on IT and business projects for more than 25 years.

Early in his career the author worked in IT for software houses in the UK, after which he completed 20 years in Financial Services IT. In the last few years he has worked independently, advising on and building websites, and founding an online ticketing platform.

His career has taken him all over the world and given him substantial experience working remotely and hiring staff to work remotely. The author has been engaged in the offshoring and outsourcing of activities since 1998, which has given him valuable insights into managing projects and managing staff remotely.

The author can be contacted from his website:
https://cliveverrall.com/contact

https://cliveverrall.com/contact/

Find out more about the author and his current book projects at https://cliveverrall.com/books

~~~

27. Acknowledgements

The author would like to express his gratitude to the following people for spending their time reviewing the book and providing comprehensive feedback. Without their good will, patience and hard work this book would not be as it is today.

Ashok Menon – India

Ian Vellosa – United Kingdom

Jeff Jue – Thailand

Nigel Burton – China

Romilly Cocking – United Kingdom

Sameeran Jenna – India

Shashikant Bhushan – Singapore

~~~

28. Other books by this author

Achieve Personal Success in Enterprise IT Offshoring, Outsourcing and Captive Centre Management

By Clive Verrall

You may be involved in offshoring today, your employer may have told you it is planning to offshore or you may have been asked to evaluate a company's strategy which includes offshoring. You may have heard that offshoring saved one organisation millions of dollars but simultaneously another organisation is mysteriously reducing its outsourcing. But what does it really mean and are these subjects comparable?

Offshoring is a huge subject. It has its own vocabulary and its own set of specific skills which are not part of the mainstream. It has its own models and life cycles. It is a product of the "flat world" and the interconnected global economy that we now live in. If you want to understand the practicalities of this subject in order to ensure your own personal success in offshoring, outsourcing, building an offshore centre, or in setting IT strategy or you are just curious about lifting the lid on this vast subject then this book will help you.

The book will focus on the offshoring of IT activities from corporate IT departments to their own offshore facilities or to an outsourcing vendor. It will also give examples of how this extends to cover non-IT Business Process Offshoring activities. This book includes advice and lessons learnt from real offshoring experiences. This is not a book about statistical trends in offshoring or untested management theory.

https://www.amazon.co.uk/Personal-Enterprise-Offshoring-Outsourcing-Management-ebook/dp/B00WGFD8TC

https://www.amazon.co.uk/Personal-Enterprise-Offshoring-Outsourcing-Management-ebook/dp/B00WGFD8TC

Essential introduction to Investment Banking Information Technology

By Clive Verrall

What do you need to know to become successful in investment banking IT? How does investment banking IT work, what are the essential concepts and the critical IT systems? This book is aimed at anyone in IT who wants to increase their understanding of the rewarding world of investment banking IT. It will be of benefit both to people who know very little about investment banking and want a complete introduction to gain entry and it will also be useful to those who already have experience and want to get a robust understanding of the subject to accelerate their career.

Investment banking is a complicated collection of subjects. It is no surprise that the IT systems built for investment banking can also be complicated and are often implemented only by people who have an in-depth understanding of a particular niche of the investment banking business for which the system is needed. This in-depth knowledge takes years to accumulate and as a result IT staff with that knowledge are hard to find and are well paid. This makes it difficult for new comers to break into this large and still growing IT area or even to switch domains within a bank once they have already started. In this book I will share my experiences gained over more than 20 years to fast track the reader's career.

Throughout the book investment banking activities are explained in the context of what their demands on the IT department are. For each activity area this includes looking at system diversity, IT team sizes, IT process maturity, technologies used, key IT roles and whether advanced mathematical skills are needed.

https://www.amazon.co.uk/Inside-Information-Technology-Tier-Investment-ebook/dp/B01FP7N50E

https://www.amazon.co.uk/Inside-Information-Technology-Tier-Investment-ebook/dp/B01FP7N50E

Find out more about this book and other books by this author at

http://www.cliveverrall.com/author.htm

https://cliveverrall.com/books/

https://cliveverrall.com/books/

~~

www.ingramcontent.com/pod-product-compliance
Lightning Source LLC
Chambersburg PA
CBHW031627210526
45464CB00004B/1784